Daniel Cohen is the Founder and CEO
of Graduway, the leading provider of alumni
networking and mentoring platforms with
clients across 30 countries.

Daniel is recognized as a leading thinker, writer
and speaker in alumni relations and was
recently recognized by LinkedIn as one of their
Top Influencers in Education.

Daniel also chairs the bi-annual Global Leaders
Summit, a gathering of global executives to
discuss best practice and strategic trends in
alumni relations.

Table of Contents

Introduction

I realize that calling this book 'The Alumni Revolution' is a dramatic title. The word revolution usually conjures up images of some sort of seismic occurrence or a powerful date with a clear 'before' and 'after'.

Whilst not on a par with the likes of the Russian or French revolutions, I do believe that what we are experiencing in the world of alumni relations is nonetheless, revolutionary.

If you take a step back and look at the number of factors that have changed in keeping in touch with our alumni today, the cumulative differences are quite dramatic.

This book comprises a series of bite-size essays on key topics that have led us to this revolution. You can read it from start to finish, or dip in and out depending on what area you are working on.

The book is aimed at schools, colleges, universities or any organization looking to connect with their alumni. For the purposes of simplicity, I have used the generic term 'school' throughout much of the book.

Chapter One deals with defining your value proposition. This is the basics. Schools used to be the central conduit for everything to do with alumni. Today, alumni no longer need the school office to connect with one another. This challenges schools. What is the core value that you bring to alumni that no one else does? Why do they need you?

Chapter Two covers building the right culture. This is for the many schools who have understood that their alumni are their most important asset, may want to benefit through increased giving, whether financial or otherwise, but don't know where to begin. This section addresses how you can build a culture of giving very quickly, even if your organization doesn't have a history of it.

Chapter Three is about engaging alumni the right way. This requires a fundamental rethink to fit the times we are living in now, and offers tips on the best ways schools can engage their network.

Chapter Four focuses on harnessing the power of social networks. We need to not just pay lip service to the likes of Facebook and LinkedIn, but know how to leverage them in our core offering. Schools need to reach out to where their alumni work, rest and play.

Chapter Five is called 'Thinking Out of the Box'. This covers strategic issues and general trends in education, and more specifically, where alumni relations are headed.

Finally, Chapter Six will help you to avoid classic mistakes – for those just creating an alumni function, and for others who may be entrenched in bad habits. This covers examples of best practice.

I would love to hear your feedback on the ideas contained in this book – do get in touch with me at Daniel.Cohen@graduway.com. I look forward to hearing from you!

Daniel Cohen

3rd February 2016.

Chapter 1 – Defining Your Value Proposition

The 'What's In It for Me?' Alumni Test

Are education institutions in denial about their alumni engagement?

Schools are implementing a variety of activities, yet are they actually making progress towards their stated goal of engaging alumni? Perhaps, they have lost sight of the basics.

Engaging alumni should not be complicated. Fundamentally it is about providing alumni with a compelling reason to engage with your institution.

Let's switch roles for a moment, and put yourself into the shoes of your alumni, and ask the most critical question, *What's In It For Me (WIIFM)?*

What is my school *uniquely* providing *today* that is of significant *value* to my life?

Uniquely? Providing a value proposition that no one else can.

Today? The provision is real time, today, and not simply a nostalgic reliance on the past.

Value? Something that I tangibly see as a valuable benefit. Maybe quantifiable in monetary terms as something for which I would have even been prepared to pay to have access.

Understanding and articulating your value proposition to alumni lies at the heart of alumni engagement.

It can be daunting to answer the WIIFM question, but it is the first serious step to developing an effective engagement strategy.

The good news is that every education institution has the potential to provide a meaningful value proposition.

Your school can uniquely give access to an exclusive alumni network that will provide your alumni with both professional and social opportunities.

Professional opportunities can be about providing access to a career community, willing and able to help make introductions, mentor one another, and even provide job opportunities.

Social opportunities that allow your alumni to join an exclusive social network that may well stretch across the world.

Each institution will express this value proposition in their own unique way.

There was media coverage this week of a school understanding and articulating their unique value proposition. Azusa Pacific University's (APU) has launched a spiritual as well as professional mentoring platform. APU has given a clear answer to the WIIFM question by providing alumni with access to receive and volunteer for valuable opportunities.

Has your school articulated a value proposition that you would be able to share?

What was the biggest challenge you faced in answering the WIIFM question?

The Engagement Matrix - How Do You Score?

If you are being really honest, how would you score your institution's level of on-line engagement?

More importantly, do you understand why you are achieving the engagement levels that you are with your alumni?

Alongside being easy to access and use, there are two critical ingredients needed for engagement: (a) strong brand and (b) valuable content.

The on-line engagement equation is a simple one:

Brand x Content equals Engagement (BC = E).

The Engagement Matrix below categorizes the different levels of alumni engagement based upon an institution's content and brand value scores.

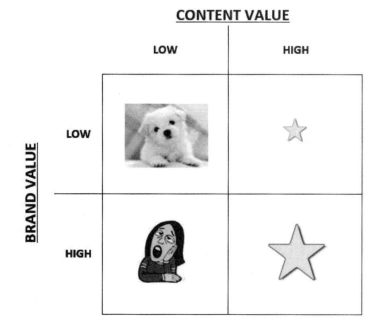

Often the engagement outcome is very intuitive. For example, in the education world, a school that has a world class brand AND is providing access to world class content will result in, unsurprisingly, relatively high alumni engagement, as per the matrix - a 'big star'. Think of the Harvards and Oxfords of this world as examples.

At the other extreme, a school with a weak brand AND providing weak content will result in relatively low engagement. As per the matrix - a 'dog'. Again no surprises here.

However where it gets interesting is when a school is not in the luxurious position of having **both** these core ingredients but has to choose to focus on just **one**.

Which should you focus on delivering first, exclusive content or brand power?

To try and answer this question, Graduway took a sample of 43 alumni networking platforms in the education space, with over 40,000 users.

Graduway correlated both the brand power and content being provided with the resulting level of engagement.

The <u>brand</u> value for each school was set at High (8), Medium (6) or Low (4) based upon school rankings. The higher the rank, the higher the brand value.

The <u>content</u> value for each school was set at High (8), Medium (6) or Low (4) based upon the number of jobs, events and news items posted by the school each week.

Finally, for each of the 43 platforms the level of on-line engagement was measured by the number of engagement acts per 100 users for the previous 30 days. This included the number of discussions, comments and photos on each platform.

In the matrix below you will see the average level of engagement with different levels of brand and content values across these 43 networks.

CONTENT VALUE

BRAND VALUE	High	Medium	Low
High	1615%	1029%	n/a
Medium	1395%	757%	355%
Low	815%	668%	189%

The analysis shows consistently that the engagement was highest where content was chosen over brand. For example a medium ranked brand with high valued content (1395%), performed stronger than a high ranked brand with medium content (1029%).

It seems clear that a school, if given the choice, should prefer improving its content value over its brand value.

The implications are significant as it may well mean changing your institution's focus toward providing higher quality content over direct brand building. Furthermore, schools cannot necessarily blame the quality of the brands they have inherited with the low levels of engagement they are achieving.

Stronger content will lead to better engagement. And guess what, with that better content and engagement, the virtuous cycle will in turn lead to you building a stronger brand.

Do you agree that content ultimately will always trump brand value? And do you have experience of building a brand via the provision of better content?

The Case for Mentoring

The provision of mentors to students and alumni used to be a low priority for education institutions.

A service offered by the careers department to the few.

Simply put, it was a 'nice to have'.

Not anymore.

Mentoring is fast being recognized as perhaps one of the most, if not the most, critical components of our formal education experience, and key in driving the long term success for college alumni.

At last week's CAAE Institute Winter Meeting in Scottsdale Arizona, I had the privilege of hearing a remarkable presentation by Brandon Busteed, the Executive Director Education and Workforce Development for Gallup, of a study commissioned with Purdue University. Brandon outlined what drives long-term alumni success and the role alumni organizations can have in impacting graduates' well-being.

You can download the full report at http://products.gallup.com/168857/gallup-purdue-index-inaugural-national-report.aspx and also see an excellent article by Brandon on their findings. For anyone working in a University, I don't think it gets more fundamental than improving the long-term well-being (both socially and financially) of their graduates.

The Gallup-Purdue study found that **where** you went to college matters less to your work life and well-being after graduation than **how** you went to college.

In particular, the study found that students being 'emotionally supported' during college improved the chances of them being engaged in their work more than two-fold, and the chances of thriving in their well-being more than three-fold. Moreover one of the most important ways to be emotionally supported is by having 'had a mentor who encouraged their goals and dreams.'

Just 22% of respondents could answer affirmatively that they had access to such a mentor. As Brandon put it,

Feeling supported and having deep learning experiences during college means everything when it comes to long-term outcomes after college. Unfortunately, not many

graduates receive a key element of that support while in college: having a mentor. And this is perhaps the biggest blown opportunity in the history of higher ed.

So why are schools not providing mentors?

Firstly, there has been a general lack of awareness of the importance of mentoring.

Secondly, schools tend to think about facilitating mentoring in very resource heavy and unscalable ways. The careers department will typically manually match and connect individuals to each other. This takes up a lot of time and is obviously not suitable if you need to do this for thousands of students.

The answer lies in a combination of leveraging your alumni and technology.

Your alumni are a readily available army of experienced and motivated mentors willing to help and guide your students. In fact you probably only need around 5-10% of your alumni to volunteer to have more mentors than you need.

Technology has also changed meaning that you can literally provide alumni mentoring platforms within days and enable students and alumni to choose and connect with each other.

The onus will clearly still remain on students to take advantage of the mentoring opportunities being made available to them. However let's at least provide that opportunity to all of our students.

Moreover, I believe there is an argument that facilitating mentoring should be seen as a life-long service offered to students and senior alumni alike.

The case for mentoring seems clear. How will schools respond to this opportunity?

Do you agree with the case for schools to provide mentors?

Do you have experience of implementing such a provision and what were your biggest challenges?

Do Your Alumni Still Need You?

The digital revolution is changing every industry. The world of education, and in particular advancement is not exempt from this change.

At the recent Graduway Global Leaders Summit, held at the Said Business School, Oxford University, **Andrew Gossen**, Senior Director for Social Media Strategy, Alumni Affairs & Development at Cornell University, gave a rather brilliant and insightful presentation. His speech entitled, *"Coping with digital disruption in higher ed advancement"* showed how digital technology has challenged almost existentially the role of the advancement profession. Click on the video below to see the full recording of Andrew's presentation.

Andrew argues that the digital revolution has massively changed how people connect and share with each other, where they spend their time, and critically how much information they can access. This is resulting in the removal of traditional intermediary functions in most industries including higher education.

One of the intermediaries who potentially is most in danger, is the alumni professional.

The three core disciplines of advancement - namely communications, alumni affairs and fundraising have all been challenged by the digital revolution. Schools no longer have a monopoly on alumni data, and hence they have lost significant control over the alumni relations function. Alumni can find each other and organize themselves without going via their school. An official institutional voice is no longer necessarily present in alumni relations!

These changes are clearly a threat to the traditional role of an alumni professional. However, they are also a massive opportunity.

In short, the role of the alumni professional appears to be changing from direct content provider, to one of a facilitator.

For communication and alumni affairs, this could be about facilitating alumni to professionally network with one another, mentor one another, without the school being administratively involved. On the social side, it could simply be enabling your alumni to create their own events via your official platform.

For fundraising - this could potentially be about better leveraging the crowd as Andrew showed with Cornell's early experience from crowd-funding.

Facilitating. Leveraging. Enabling. Accelerating. These will be the core skills for alumni professionals in the future.

The digital revolution is changing the world and will continue to do so. It's time for alumni professionals to embrace that change.

Do you agree that the alumni professional's role needs to change?

Are bigger changes required in communication and alumni affairs than in fund-raising?

What do you see as the biggest threat and opportunity from the digital revolution?

Is It Time To Make Alumni Pay?

When it comes to students, education institutions seem to understand the principles of charging for a quality service. However when it comes to alumni, they seem to lose their way.

I am surprised that many schools I speak with, particularly outside of continental Europe, still do not charge their alumni membership dues to be part of their network and organization.

Yes, I understand that students have already paid when they were on campus, and typically a significant minority will continue to make donations once they graduate. I also understand that this also touches on a separate issue about the independence of alumni associations. But for many schools, it is clear that the majority of alumni do not pay anything.

Chris Marshall, Vice President at Grenzebach Glier and Associates, confirmed for me recently that in his view the vast majority of US institutions do not charge alumni to be members and the number of dues paying alumni associations is actually shrinking each year.

This in my view does not sound like a healthy way to build a vibrant alumni community. The question is why should alumni membership be 'free'? And is the fact that it is free causing disengagement?

Let's look at the for-profit world for an alternative model.

What do you think as a consumer when someone offers you a free product? Is this something that you typically value over the long term? Normally if you do value it, then you are prepared to pay for the product either with money or with your data and time (e.g. Facebook, YouTube). One way or another you pay something.

Moreover I don't think organizations that have a quality alumni product need to fear charging for access to it.

L'Oreal and Stella Artois are two brands that I admire that have done an outstanding job in positioning themselves as quality premium products.

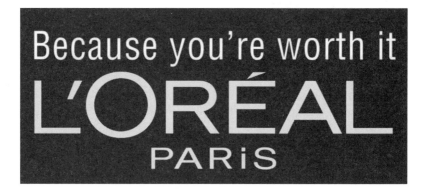

Were consumers scared off by L'Oreal's 'Because I am worth it' slogan or Stella's 'Reassuringly expensive'? Absolutely not. On the contrary it helped build their trust and value score.

Consumers are smart and over the long term will give their loyalty and support to those companies who provide and yes, charge for a quality offering.

In the for-profit world, 'free' is rarely valued, and I think in the not-for-profit world, we have a similar outcome.

My hypothesis here is that consistently charging all alumni membership dues, could be a driver of greater engagement.

Buy-in comes from those who have 'skin in the game'. A trusted and exclusive network would probably be even more appreciated and valued if all alumni actually were asked to pay a fee to be part of that network. When you tell your alumni that being a member is 'free', what are you communicating about your brand?

Moreover, by charging alumni, we start to put a healthy focus on the value proposition offered by schools to their alumni. Is your school offering a sufficiently strong value offering to your alumni to justify charging, and if not, what is missing?

Finally, I think in addition to greater engagement and participation by alumni, the idea that the alumni association should be funded not just by a few wealthy donors but my the alumni mass, brings a healthy dose of democratization to the running of schools.

In summary, this may be the proverbial chicken and egg question. Schools need to probably have both better engagement programs and in parallel to potentially charge for them. What do you think?

Do you think all alumni should be charged dues to be a member of the network?

Do you have experience of introducing alumni dues and what was the impact on participation and engagement rates afterwards?

To what extent do schools need to change their value offering and engagement programs to be able to justify charging alumni?

Disgruntled Alumni. Can You Afford to Ignore Them?

Unhappy customers are bad for business, every business.

In the education world, there appears to be a proportion of customers (i.e. alumni) who are not satisfied with their purchase. And the scary thing about unhappy customers is that they can shout very loudly.

Nicole Matejic shouted very loudly this week in her intriguing blog that shone a light right into the heart of the education world. Her blog entitled an ''Open letter to the Vice Chancellor of the University of New England'' is well worth a read if you have not yet had the chance to do so. In this open letter Nicole described what she felt when being solicited for money from an institution that she had not been in touch with for almost a decade.

Nicole was clearly unhappy with her school's approach. Whether in her individual circumstances she was justified to feel the way she did or not, and whether the blog was the right medium or not to raise the issue are interesting points, but not ones that I want to pass judgment on here.

Rather, I would like to focus on the sizeable reaction to the blog.

When you read through the 60+ comments to her blog, you can see that opinion among alumni seems clearly divided on the virtue of giving money to your alma mater.

To quote two comments on Nicole's blog that seemed to epitomize the divided opinion;

1. I think your letter is unfair. It is not unreasonable to ask graduates for funds every now and then, given that you benefited enormously from your education.

versus

2. I'm not giving my old uni a cent! They ripped us off when we were there and have the nerve to ask for more money!!

What is clear is that there does appear to be a significant percentage of alumni that feel something close to sentiment (2.) How many alumni feel like that is impossible to tell and will vary by country and type of institution. But even if just a small minority, wouldn't schools be foolish to ignore them and risk the damaging noise of disgruntled customers?

So why do some alumni feel so let down and critically, what can schools do to make the situation better?

Well my hypothesis is that there is one major cause for this alumni discontent. The problem rests on the fact that alumni appear no longer to see as positive return on their investment (in pure career terms) as was once expected. In fairness this could be due to unrealistic expectations in the first place and also a changing employment market.

However it may also be due to the fact that schools in general are not doing enough to assist their graduates and alumni in progressing in their chosen career. For example how well are schools facilitating mentor relationships, networking within specific professional affinities, or providing access to real employment opportunities? It may also be that schools are doing these things but not communicating them loudly or clearly enough.

Schools needs to better both communicate their value, and also critically do a better job in providing their graduates with tangible day to day value in their careers.

Offer real life-long value to alumni and I believe letters like these will be a thing of the past.

Do you agree that schools need to improve the value they offer their alumni?

Are there other causes and solutions to alumni discontent? What % of alumni do you think have this level of discontent?

And finally, what should schools be doing to provide better value to their graduates?

'What Women Want' Alumni Thinking - Part 1

Last week I was watching that classic romantic comedy, 'What Women Want' – for the rest of the article referred to as 'W-W-W'.

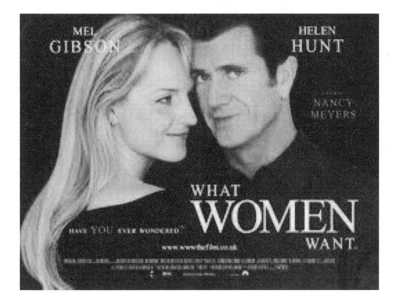

For those of you who missed out the first time around, the movie's central character is Nick Marshall (played by Mel Gibson) who is a chauvinist advertising executive whose understanding of women is limited to figuring out how to seduce them.

One day, he has an accident in his bathroom and receives an electric shock that results in him obtaining the unusual ability to hear for the first time exactly what women are thinking and hence what they really want.

At the movie's core is the often dysfunctional relationship between men and women and in particular men's apparent inability to understand and give women what they really want.

Yet it provoked me into thinking about other dysfunctional relationships including, in my world, the school-alumni relationship.

Like with men, it seems clear to everyone 'What Schools Want' - and they are usually only after one thing! But the key question should be 'What do Alumni Really Want'?

Does your school truly apply the 'W-W-W' approach to relations with alumni and think first about 'What Alumni Want' before asking them to give back?

Giving alumni what they really want is about understanding the value proposition your school is offering.

If your value proposition is weak, can you really expect alumni to stay in touch and want to give back?

The value proposition to alumni cannot be limited to just reminiscing about their historical experiences of studying at your institution. A real value proposition is one where the school makes an important contribution both professionally and socially throughout the lives of alumni, from graduation to grave.

Understanding what your alumni really want is your school's critical first step to transforming your relationship with them.

'What Women Want' Alumni Thinking - Part 2

In Part 1 of *'"What Women Want' Alumni Thinking"* I started to delve into the often dysfunctional relationship between schools and alumni. Just like Mel Gibson who played a character that completely misunderstood 'What Women Want', so too it appeared many schools were unable to truly understand 'What *Alumni* Want'. Here in Part 2 of this article, I provide practical advice on identifying what alumni really want.

Paramount

Schools have a huge opportunity to transform their relationship with their alumni if they can better think about

'What *Alumni* Want' *before* asking them to give back. Giving alumni what they really want starts by understanding the value proposition your school is offering.

The value proposition to alumni cannot be limited to just reminiscing about their historical experiences of studying at your institution. *A real value proposition is one where the school makes an important contribution both professionally and socially throughout the lives of alumni, from graduation to grave.*

So how do you create a real value proposition for your alumni?

The key ingredient you must have is **exclusivity**. You need to ask yourself what can your school *uniquely* offer your alumni that they simply cannot get elsewhere?

And before you say it, exclusivity is not a commodity that is limited to Ivy League schools, but is something every school can generate over time.

Your alumni are part of an exclusive network, an exclusive membership, an exclusive club. The more you demonstrate the value of being part of that network, the more exclusive it will become. This is about building and leveraging the value of your school brand.

Practically, your alumni network has the potential to be both an exclusive *professional* network and simultaneously an exclusive *social* network.
An exclusive professional network? – Yes – by providing your alumni with unique opportunities such as mentoring, employment, membership of a network that is willing and able to help, and access to continuous professional development and education.

An exclusive social network? – Again Yes – by providing your alumni with exclusive social opportunities that they simply cannot get elsewhere - the ability to meet new friends and reminisce with old ones only because of your school and their shared connection.

Every school has the ability to provide its alumni with exclusive professional and social opportunities. Every school can offer a value proposition to their alumni that begins to give them what they really want. Start giving your alumni what they really want, and see how this transforms your alumni relationship.

In the final part of this article published next week, I will be providing practical advice on critically *how* to make these exclusive opportunities more *accessible* to your alumni.

'What Women Want' Alumni Thinking - Part 3

In Part 1 of *"What Women Want' Alumni Thinking"* I started to delve into the often dysfunctional relationship between schools and alumni. Just like Mel Gibson who played a character that completely misunderstood 'What Women Want', so too it appeared many schools were unable to truly understand 'What *Alumni* Want'.

In Part 2, I provided practical advice on identifying what alumni really want by showing how schools can build an **exclusive** value proposition for their alumni; where schools are able to demonstrate the unique value both professionally and socially of being part of their exclusive network.

In this final part of this article, I will be providing practical advice on critically how to

make these exclusive opportunities
more *accessible* for your alumni.

So you now have identified and implemented a
real value proposition for your alumni -
exclusive professional and social opportunities
that your school can uniquely provide. Great
first step. However, although this is a necessary
first step, it is still not sufficient in giving
alumni what they really want. What's missing?

The answer is making that value proposition **easily accessible** to your alumni is almost as critical as the value proposition itself. There is a truism that most schools will relate to. When your alumni change jobs or move location, who are they more likely to inform – Facebook or your school? For most alumni it is the former.

This example starts to allude to the fact that schools need to find ways to stay better connected to their alumni by providing their unique value on the alumni's terms and not just their own.

There are two key elements of accessibility that a school needs to address.

1. Social Networks – contrary to popular belief this is not about a school being on every possible social network out there from Facebook, to LinkedIn, Instagram, Pinterest, Twitter etc. I think for most alumni the real engagement on a school's social network is relatively low even if they like you, follow you or join you! What does 20,000 likes on your Facebook page really translate to in the world of advancement?

Rather the value of Social Networks is in the fact that it is the eco-system in which your alumni use and are familiar with. Their contact information is up-dated there, it's their social and professional identity on-line, they find these social networks intuitive to use and it's their virtual place for storing all of their lists of friends and professional contacts. *The better a school can integrate Social Networks into their offering, the easier it will be for alumni to be engaged and access your value proposition.*

2. Anytime, anywhere – your alumni need to be able to access your exclusive offering literally anytime and anywhere. This means that your value proposition needs to be accessible on-line, and not just web but obviously mobile as well.

Moreover your offering needs to be available on any device, anywhere.

In conclusion, irrespective of how exclusive your value offering is, if it is not easily accessible by your alumni then it becomes much less valuable.

Having said that, being accessible to your alumni on social networks and any device is also not a substitute for offering a real value proposition. You need both.

The secret to giving alumni what they really want, is giving them an exclusive value offering, yet one that is easily accessible. Your school needs to be present and easily accessible in the lives of alumni, from graduation to grave, offering them unique professional and social opportunities along the way. Give your alumni what they want, and start to see the positive impact on your relationship.

Chapter Two – Building the Right Culture

Who 'Owns' the Alumni?
Careers or Alumni Relations?

There are a number of key stakeholders that have an important say in the relationship between an education institution and their alumni; Career Services, Development, Alumni Relations, Communication, Marketing and Admissions to name but a few.

However there are two departments where at times I see some professional tension over alumni, namely Career Services and Alumni Relations.

I believe this tension is driven by two different viewpoints on student-alumni interactions.

Career Services is understandably focused on the student. In particular how to help students enter the career of their choice while using alumni as an important resource along the way for mentoring, internships and employment.

Alumni Relations on the other hand is focused on the wider alumni body. Graduating students, although an important segment, will only make up around 5% of their total alumni. Their focus is much more on how best to engage *all* alumni and provide them with a valuable career and social community.

In short, for Careers Services alumni are a resource, a means to an end. For Alumni Relations they are the end.

These two legitimate yet different philosophies regarding alumni can create professional tension if not managed properly.

Moreover ultimately the danger of these tensions is the negative impact on alumni through miscommunication and duplication. Neither department wants to alienate what is both a valuable resource and an important end customer.

So how to get the balance right?

Here comes the controversial bit.

I believe some schools solve this tension through compromising between the two departments without ever properly defining who has the actual ownership on communication with alumni. The approach could be described as *'let's both own interactions with alumni and try hard to coordinate where possible.'*
I think this approach is a mistake.

It results in duplicate systems, confusion, wasted money, and suboptimal student-alumni relations.

Even worse, what if alumni start to feel like a resource rather than a customer in their own right?

I believe schools need to clearly define who owns alumni. I also believe that it should be Alumni Relations.

At the end of the day, the alumni are the more important partner in the student-alum relationship. Students are the ones who need something from the relationship (contacts, introductions, advice, etc). Alumni are there simply to give back and help.

As such the focus needs to be on:

- making the relationship as easy and straightforward for alumni as possible

- all communication to alumni should come via Alumni Relations

- the home for student-alum interactions should be the alumni portal (and not a student centric one!)

Alumni Relations need to own the alumni relationship in order that it always remains a healthy resource for everyone, including Career Services.

Who do you think should 'own' the alumni relationship?

Making the Case for Funding Alumni Relations

The education world is under pressure.

Public funding is falling. Tuition fees are rising. Cost cutting is everywhere.

Yet I hear consistently from Alumni Relations professionals of how they are under-resourced in terms of both headcount and budget. In fact some would go as far as to claim that Alumni Relations is the most under-resourced department.

In such a tough macro environment making the case for increasing Alumni Relations funding is a challenge.

Speak to your Dean or Vice-Chancellor about increasing Alumni Relations funding and you may get a standard response that surely there are other more pressing and urgent areas for investment than Alumni Relations?

We seem unable to articulate clearly enough that Alumni Relations is an urgent priority and not a 'nice to have'.

I think there are two main reasons why we are failing:

1. **Short-term thinking** - education institutions need results quickly from investments they make. Building your brand through your ambassadors is critical to the long term health of the school.
2. **Measuring the wrong things** - the key performance indicators for leaders in education are usually student numbers, research or teachings scores and not direct alumni relations measures.

So what can be done?

One route is to rehash our old arguments of how Alumni Relations will improve enrollment figures, allow the selling of more executive education services, and of course lead to greater donations.

However I think it time for us to be a little more direct. The old arguments are falling on deaf ears.

Instead, one measure your Leadership will surely listen to concerns ranking.

The good news is that the major external rankings are increasingly putting greater emphasis on alumni feedback.

For example, Bloomberg Businessweek requires 30% of its class to respond even before making it on their rankings. The Financial Times alumni responses contribute a staggering 59% of their ranking's weight.

So in short, when you are making that proposal to increase Alumni Relations funding... yes, talk about the long-term health of the school and yes talk about enrollment and development.

But let's be smarter. Let's talk about the short-term impact on rankings as well as the long-term brand building that will come from investing more in Alumni Relations.

Do Schools Practice What They Teach?

Once upon a time, there was a former student who approached the Dean of his old school for some advice.

"Nice to see you", said the Dean. "If I am not mistaken, I don't think we have spoken to each other since you graduated all those years ago."

"It is nice to see you too", said the former student. "Mr Dean, if you don't mind, I wanted to get your professional opinion on the state of my business."

"Sure", replied the Dean.

"Well, something is missing in my business, and I can't put my finger on what is going wrong", replied the former student. "Indeed a recent industry survey ranked my company way down and I am at a loss as to what to do."

"I see", said the Dean, "please tell me a little about your business."

"My business seems to have all the right fundamentals in place as you taught me" replied the former student. "I work in the professional services industry and rigorously applied the '7Ps' to our marketing mix. We have a high quality product, we charge a premium price..."

"I see", said the Dean. "And what happens after your customers have bought and consumed your product? What interactions do you have with them?"

"To be honest," replied the former student, "Very little."

"Well, the underlying problem seems clear to me," replied the Dean. "You are neglecting one of your most important assets – your former customers. Fix that and you will fix your business."

"Thank you so much", replied the former student.

"My pleasure", said the Dean. "And next time don't leave it so many years before getting back in touch!"

The next morning over breakfast, the Dean opened up the Financial Times to review the latest school rankings. He scratched his head at a loss as to what he should do about the poor showing of his school. He could not put his finger on it. Where was his school going wrong?

Unfair story? Maybe. But you get my point. In general schools are not practicing what they teach when it comes to their former customers, their alumni.

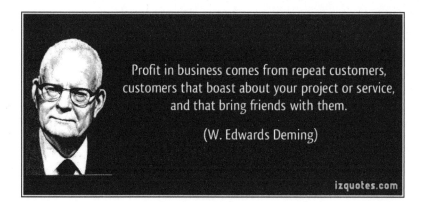

Profit in business comes from repeat customers, customers that boast about your project or service, and that bring friends with them.

(W. Edwards Deming)

izquotes.com

Schools cannot afford to ignore their alumni. Let me show you why with **the '8Rs'.**

1. **Repeat** – it is significantly easier to get old customers to repeat a purchase than to attract new customers. Schools often have executive education programs to offer whether within the institution or providing it in-house within the company of an alum. Staying in touch with your alumni will result in repeat business.

2. **Referrals** – when selecting which school a prospective student should apply to, how important is the referral of an alum who has studied at that school? What percentage of your applications each year was generated by the referral of an alum?

3. **References** – being able to use your alumni as references to the quality and value of your school is incredibly important. This can also be done informally to show the career outcomes of studying at your institution.

4. **Reviewing** – many schools use their alumni not just to recommend new applicants but to take an active role in the recruitment process by interviewing and reviewing prospective students.

5. **Recruitment** - your alumni are a valuable source of improving your career offering by mentoring, networking and employing your students.

6. **Receiving** – donations are a potentially lucrative source of funding for your institution.

7. **Rankings** - for virtually all of the major rankings, schools need to be able to provide alumni to be

interviewed and ideally with a glowing reference. If you are not in touch with your alumni, how can you expect your ranking to be good?

8. **Reputation** – in the final analysis a school is only as good as the alumni it produces. Your alumni are mini reflections of your brand and one worthy of you investing your resources to support.

There is a huge opportunity in the world of education for schools to invest in finding their alumni and re-engaging them. Forget the '7Ps'- it is time to start thinking about the '8Rs' and what your engaged alumni could do for your school.

Is your school missing an opportunity with your alumni?

What are the barriers stopping you engaging your alumni and benefiting from the '8 Rs' immediately?

Ask Alumni for Money? No Way.

Many schools outside of the United States, and in particular in Europe, could be described as being 'skeptical' when it comes to fundraising from their alumni.

On the one hand they know the funding model of education is changing with the balance moving away from public funding towards alumni giving.

On the other hand, while many American schools feel comfortable fundraising for the worthy cause of education, most European schools appear awkward in soliciting funds from their alumni.

If I had asked a European school a year or two ago if they solicit alumni - the typical response would be a shrug that things are a little different on this side of the Atlantic!

Simply put, I think most European schools until recently felt they had neither the will nor the ability to create a culture of giving similar to that which exists in the United States.

Times are changing.

Melissa Korn in the Wall Street Journal, wrote an intriguing piece a few months ago on the changing culture in European business schools towards fundraising. And I see that change in my day to day interactions with schools. Schools in virtually every country in the world are realizing that they need to take a more serious interest in their alumni. Maybe not to solicit large funds today, but to begin to lay the foundations for tomorrow and to build critically the culture for future giving.

Elise Betz, Executive Director of Alumni
Relations from the University of Pennsylvania
recently gave an inspiring key note speech at
the Graduway Global Leaders Summit. Her talk
entitled *"Cultivating Roots: Building a Culture of
Student Philanthropy and Engagement"* was a
bold example of how a school (albeit a top one),
can strategically invest in their culture of giving
with an eye on the very long term.

It may take some time, but I am convinced that
someone will turn around 20 years from now
and bless Elise for the work she and the
leadership at Penn did in investing in their
philanthropic culture.

It is well worth watching in full Elise's keynote
to see how she installed a tradition and culture
of giving. I took away three critical ingredients
that were needed to make this 'new' culture
stick.

Firstly, to get students involved in this culture of philanthropy while still on campus - approaching them once they graduate is clearly too late!

Secondly, to have not just the support but the active participation of the leadership of the University in the campaign to build that culture.

Finally, the determination, innovation and perseverance to get the new traditions and customs to stick. As Elise memorably articulated, schools need to stick to the line that 'this is what we do here' when helping to bed down the new culture - 'a new tradition only takes two years to create!'

I am a believer. I am convinced that if any school, and I mean any school, is determined enough, they could also build a culture of philanthropy and engagement.

Do you have experience of building such a culture in your institution? What would you advise others to do?

What remains the biggest obstacle in making a new culture of giving stick in your institution?

Do you agree that every school has the potential to create a philanthropic culture?

Does Your School Pass the Red Socks Test?

The University of Phoenix aired this slick commercial some time ago. It's brilliant in many ways. Concise. Clear. Catchy.

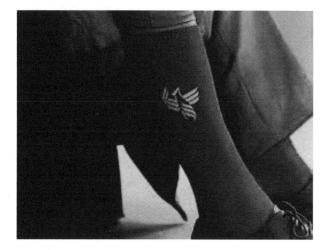

Schools often focus on connecting students with alumni. This is one of the best examples I have seen of a school leveraging the connection between *prospective students and* **alumni**. Take a look for yourself.

Having watched the commercial, I think there is a two-part test that arises. Let's see how your school scores on this 'Red Socks' test.

1. Do you have a clear return on investment rationale for prospective students?
It doesn't matter how famous your institution is, prospective students and their parents will want to hear a clear case that making this significant investment in their education is going to pay out.

2. Are you leveraging sufficiently with prospective students, the desirability of joining your alumni network?
Every school has the ability to make its brand feel more exclusive, trusted and yes desired. This should be a critical component of your admissions strategy.

Every school should be utilizing its alumni in the recruitment of new students. This is not limited to involving them in the interviewing and screening process. More importantly it's about building an exclusive and trusted brand which can only be done through the full partnership of your alumni.

Schools conduct 'campaigns' aimed at their alumni all the time. Yet it may sound obvious but have you ever put yourself in the 'receiving shoes' of those alumni?

Start by collating **all** the various emails and communications that your school has sent in the last few months and put them all together on one virtual table. Is the result a perfectly consistent and coherent message for your alumni? Probably not.

Chapter 3 – Engaging Alumni the Right Way

Engaging Alumni in the Wrong Order

Most professionals working with alumni for an educational institution understand that you probably need to have in place three things to effectively manage alumni on-line.

The issue is that most schools implement the three in the wrong order.

What are those 'three' and what is the 'wrong' order?

1. **Data** - schools usually build an internal database first to better manage alumni data. e.g. The Raiser's Edge, Advance, Salesforce etc.
2. **Communicate** - they then build marketing and fundraising tools to better communicate and transact

with alumni. e.g. NetCommunity, iModules, Mail Chimp etc.

3. **Engage** - finally schools build an on-line engagement platform where alumni will network and interact with each other. e.g. Graduway.

   Although all three components are necessary, they are being implemented by schools in the wrong order.

Let me explain.

Firstly Graduway's own research has shown that on average schools are missing accurate contact information (email addresses, phone numbers) for around 70% of their alumni. You are not getting the full return from your new cutting edge database if you are missing so much data. Your database is only as good as the data in it.

Secondly, the response rates to these smart marketing and fundraising tools is relatively low. Again, you are not getting the full return from these amazing tools if your alumni are disengaged and unresponsive.

It all starts and ends with alumni engagement.

If you are able to truly engage alumni by offering a valuable career network and community for your alumni, then they will reward you with two things.

Firstly, the higher engagement will lead you to have more accurate contact information in your database. The more engaged the alumni are, the more frequently their contact information will be refreshed, and the more accurate your database will become.

Secondly, higher engagement will lead you to have higher response rates from your marketing and fundraising tools. The more value alumni get from being part of your network, the more responsive and willing they will be to give back.

Better engagement will lead to better data on, and better responsiveness from, alumni.

And what to do if you cannot afford all three tools and platforms?

I would suggest that engagement should be the primary focus.

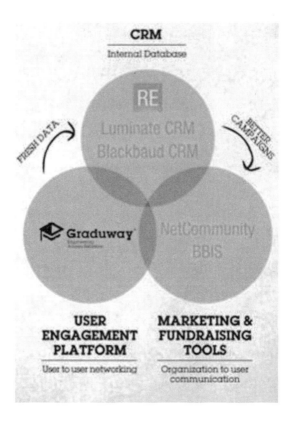

Let me conclude by showing visually how the three work together in the case of Graduway's preferred technology partnership with Blackbaud.

Engage. Data. Communicate.

Let's start engaging alumni in the right order and see the difference.

2 Golden Rules to 'Get Through' to Your Alumni

I sometimes feel we are over-complicating this whole alumni thing.

We are getting very sophisticated - accumulating lots of data, investing in hiring people, new IT systems, working extremely hard. In short we are throwing lots of resources at alumni.

But are we actually making progress in 'getting through' to our alumni?

I am *not* even talking here about *why* you want to get through to your alumni.
Institutions have different reasons as to why they want to get through to alumni - whether it's fundraising, gaining volunteers and

ambassadors, building a career community or simply providing mentors to students.

The reason why you as an institution want to get through to your alumni does *not* actually change the methodology of how best to achieve this. So let's get back to basics.

There are only two golden rules for getting through to alumni:

1. **Physically Getting Through** e.g. Do you have their correct phone number? For what percentage of your alumni do you have contactable information? My rule of thumb is that on average institutions are missing an accurate phone number or email address for around 70% of their alumni. Without fixing this basic first step, it is literally impossible to 'get through' to your alumni.

2. **Emotionally Getting Through** e.g. When you do get through to them on the phone physically, does

the alum know why you are important to them? The reason cannot be just nostalgic that they studied at your institution 20 years ago. Rather the emotional connection comes from your institution playing a *daily* role in the lives of your alumni both socially and professionally. It's an emotional connection based upon the past, present and future.

There is a simple litmus test I would challenge any Alumni Relations professional to ask themselves when looking at their initiatives - will this help you get through to your alumni better, either physically or emotionally or ideally both?

If the answer is 'no' - maybe it's time to question whether there could be a better place to invest your resources.

Applying Safari Principles to Alumni

I have just returned from an amazing family safari vacation in South Africa.

For those who have not yet witnessed the majesty of the wild animal kingdom, then I thoroughly recommend it to you. It was simply breathtaking.

What I also found fascinating was the ability of the safari to hold my children's attention which is not the easiest thing to do.

Hour after hour they were captivated by the safari experience, even when nothing particularly exciting was happening outside.

So what was it about the safari experience that held their attention? And is there anything we can we learn and apply in the Alumni Relations world, especially in how best to engage alumni?

1. **Unscripted** - this may sound obvious but there were no guarantees every time we went out on safari. Maybe we would see some of the Big 5 animals, maybe we would see nothing. The excitement of having an unscripted authentic experience where anything could happen kept them engaged. *Applying this to the Alumni Relations world, has the way we engage alumni become too predictable, stale and scripted?*

2. **Lack of control of the experience** - strangely enough my inability to control what my children were going to see made them feel more involved in the experience. The safari was their experience not my choreographed one. They were deciding which path we would go down. *How often in the Alumni world do we insist on controlling every aspect of the engagement? We are almost scared to give our*

alumni the microphone and decide what they want to talk about. Engagement requires not only a good reason to engage, but providing our alumni with the space to engage.

Do we need to rethink how we engage alumni by first making the engagement more unscripted and secondly giving our alumni more control over the conversation and its direction?

It's Alumni Engagement, Stupid.

A Senior Alumni Relations Director spelled it out for me as follows:

Daniel, there are only two basic rules of fundraising... firstly, make sure you have for every potential donor a working phone number to call. Secondly, when potential donors do answer the phone, ensure that they are sufficiently engaged, before you even call, to know exactly why you are valuable to them. That's it. Simple.

It sounds simple but I sometimes see schools misunderstanding these two basic rules and building their alumni strategy in the wrong order as follows.

They answer the first rule of fundraising by saying: yes we are missing basic contact information on our alumni, so let's build an expensive new database!

After a year and a lot of spent money, they have a beautiful new database but are unfortunately still missing basic and accurate contact information for much of their alumni body.

In short, a great database does not mean great data!

Schools then answer the second rule of fundraising by saying: yes we have unresponsive alumni, so let's build expensive new communication tools such as websites, email marketing templates and donation processing systems.

Yet great communication tools do not necessarily translate into significantly higher alumni responsiveness.

To continue our original analogy - it would be like schools investing in an expensive new phone directory and buying the latest cutting edge Apple mobile and expecting this somehow to dramatically change their fundraising outcome.

It is not how nice the phone directory looks that matters, but rather the accuracy of the information within it.

It is also not the mobile phone itself that matters, but how the call is received.

Schools seem to be investing time and money in the things that by themselves will struggle to deliver the results required.

Instead, the primary challenge in my view, should be how to maximize alumni engagement.

If alumni are engaged, then you will be rewarded with up to date contact information (whether you have a great database or not).

If alumni are engaged, then they will response positively to your communication (whether you have the latest communication tools or not).

An effective alumni strategy lives and rests on alumni engagement. Without engagement, everything else feels much less relevant.

I understand that building a new database or website fits better within all of our comfort zones and that alumni engagement is not easy to achieve. I also understand that by the time schools get around to seriously thinking about alumni engagement, most will have not much money, time or energy left.

Yet we do not have a choice. We need the focus and priorities of alumni departments to be radically changed.

Let's start with alumni engagement. Let's put significantly more resources into alumni engagement.

To misquote President Clinton, "it's alumni engagement, stupid."

What Is Your Picture of Alumni Engagement?

When it comes to alumni engagement, we often get lost in the detail.

To be more precise, we often get lost in the metrics.

There is the big question about what to measure that will capture both the 'Fund-raising' and 'Friend-raising' nature of alumni relations.

As my friend Chris Marshall from GG+A has cited to me in the past, most education institutions will actively measure engagement metrics typically centered around:

1. **Donors** - alumni that gave their money (however big or small)
2. **Attendees** - alumni that participated in an event (in person or virtually via social networks)

94

3. **Volunteers** - alumni that gave their time

   Donors. Attendees. Volunteers. There are all

   critical engagement areas and I am very

   supportive of measuring and ranking your

   individual alumni by them as well.

   Yet at the same time I also feel some schools

   may take false comfort from these metrics that

   camouflage the true status of an institution's

   alumni engagement.

   Forget the metrics for one moment, and let me

   ask you a different question.

   The old cliché that a picture is worth a thousand

   words seems appropriate here. If you were

   asked to draw a picture of your alumni

   engagement, what would it look like?

   Let me give you two examples:

1. Empty theater

This picture highlights fundamental problems with your alumni above and beyond engaging them. If this is your picture, your focus is probably on physically finding lost alumni and having the basics in place like up to date phone numbers and emails.

2. Standing in silence

This in my opinion is probably the most common picture of engagement. The basketball arena is packed with fans - literally standing room only. Yet look closely. These fans turned up, but they are standing there in complete silence. They want to be associated with you and are proud of their alma mater but have not found their voice. You probably have not provided them with the value proposition required, the motivation, to find their voice. However the potential remains huge.

The picture of what your alumni engagement currently looks like is important. It will help to focus your institution.

Yet what could be potentially even more important than your current engagement picture, is your future one. What is the vision for your institution's alumni engagement?

Draw both pictures. Draw them with your team, and you may have taken the first important step to transforming your alumni engagement.

How to Connect Emotionally with Alumni?

I hope the following simple pictorial story will resonate with you.

They graduate...

They become alumni...

They become part of a network...

Nostalgia. Emotion. Trust.

These are *not* 'nice-to-haves' but critical ingredients that will make the difference in the level of alumni engagement your institution can achieve.

When we look at our own giving, whether money or time, the organizations for which we feel a greater emotional connection will receive the lion-share of our giving.

The more emotional we feel towards an institution, the more engaged we will be: the stronger that emotion, the wider and deeper the giving.

But typically what happens after graduation?

The sad reality is that although many students will graduate with some emotional connection with their alma mater, this will fade over time.

So what can be done?

Well, the trust and emotion your alumni feel about your institution is often represented by your brand.

If we were going to rank the world's leading brands, we would come up with the usual for-profit candidates - Apple, Google, Coca-Cola, etc. However education brands would score highly if the rankings were done not on revenue, but on a more precious commodity, namely trust.

Each school has an incredibly valuable asset in its brand that needs to be properly leveraged.

The more you leverage your school brand, the greater the trust and emotion that will be generated - the greater the engagement.

Consequently, the surprise therefore is that some schools do not fully leverage their brand in their on-line engagement with alumni. This is reflected in lower engagement levels.

Research by Graduway showed, for example, that branded school platforms are on average 40 times more engaged than non-branded ones.

The more branded you can make your on-line engagement, the more the commitment of your users will be, and the greater the value of the alumni network becomes.

Is your current on-line platform branded? How consistent and holistic is that branding? And critically does the on-line experience feel like to your alumni as if 'they have come home'?

Your interactions with alumni need to be more emotional, more branded. Only then will you start to maximize alumni engagement.

Don't Be Afraid of Your Alumni

Let's face it, most Alumni Relations Directors are a little afraid of their alumni.

To some extent this is completely understandable. Unhappy alumni can be extremely vocal.

Some of you may remember an old blog of mine from a few months ago. It discussed the case of a certain alum from an Australian University who wrote a public letter on LinkedIn about how unhappy she was that her alma mater dare ask her for money when they had not been in touch for so long.

Yes, her negative blog received 10,000 views but schools must not draw the wrong conclusions from examples like this.

Let's start with two home-truths.

Firstly, it is a statistical certainty that when an education institution does any alumni engagement activity then there will be a small minority that give a negative reaction. That small minority may even give quite a vocal negative response via emails and phone calls. Despite their noise they remain small in number.

The second truth is that the vast majority of your alumni will probably *silently* be neutral at worst, and hopefully be very appreciative of your engagement activity.
Should the happy but quiet majority of your alumni be over-ruled by the loud minority?

I often find that some schools are so concerned about offending alumni and enduring their vocal response that it affects the frequency of their engagement. There is a fear about over-communicating with alumni that leads to a paralysis of engagement.

The logic almost dictates that it is better to engage less with alumni if it means reducing the risk of causing some negative reaction, however small, from a minority of alumni.

I think differently. Schools need to be more confident.

Schools need to put the vocal minority into perspective and concentrate their efforts on providing alumni engagement that adds real value to the lives of alumni.

The best answer to disgruntled alumni is to offer them engagement that is actually relevant and valuable to their lives.

Don't be afraid. Keep engaging your alumni.

Why Alumni First Impressions Matter

Imagine you are an alum who logs into their school alumni network for the very first time.

Within milliseconds, the alum realizes that it is a dead network. A ghost-town. Clearly no one has visited the site for a long time and there seems to be zero activity going on.

The alum will reach two obvious conclusions.

Firstly - there is no point contributing any content to the network (posting comments, jobs, photos etc.) as the network is dead.

Secondly - there is no point ever revisiting this network again.

I have given a name to this phenomenon - the "Law of Dead Networks".

If your first *impression* as a user of your alumni network is that it is dead, then no surprises, the network will eventually become dead with zero activity.

What matters here is not the reality of whether it is actually engaged or not, but critically the first impression of that user.

The good news is that the Law of Dead Networks also works in reverse.

If you can provide users with an initial first impression of a dynamic, engaged and active network, then this will become self-fulfilling.

The Law of Dead Networks is simple - the impression of low activity leads to low activity, while the impression of high activity leads to high activity.

Therefore the challenge for all education institutions is how to provide a world class user experience to ensure the Law of Dead Networks works for, and not against, your school.

Schools need to start thinking seriously about the UI, UX and design of their on-line platforms.

Chapter 4 – Harnessing the Power of Social Networks

Size Is Not Everything

I admit it. I am obsessed with LinkedIn and am a bit of an addict when it comes to collecting contacts.

I surpassed the milestone of 500+ contacts some time ago and am now rapidly approaching my 2,000th contact. But how valuable really is that collection of contacts?

In the social world I have heard of people clearing out all their friends on Facebook and starting again. However I have not heard of a similar experiment in the professional world. Maybe professional contacts are simply more valuable than friends!

Anyway let's imagine a doomsday scenario. You log-in one morning to LinkedIn and find that your account has been magically reset and that your 500+ contacts have disappeared and you need to start again.

What next? How long would it take you to recover the majority of the value you once had from that list of contacts?

Or to put it more directly, how many of those 500+ contacts would you need to reconnect with to deliver most of the value that you once enjoyed from your professional network?

It would seem that probably a minority of those contacts will give you the majority of that professional networking value.

There is a scientific debate about the relationship between the size of a network and its value probably most famously explained through Metcalfe's Law (See bottom of article for a link to an excellent article on the details of this scientific debate).

As your network size increases, the total value of the network probably does increase but critically by how much?

For most scientific laymen like myself, it seems obvious that **contacts are not of equal value**. Although having more contacts will increase the breadth of your networking reach, it probably is not a substitute for also having a smaller number of deeper and more helpful contacts or groups.

The future of networking will be about how two types of networking interact and co-exist in your life.

On the one hand we will continue to have these amazing networks like Facebook and LinkedIn that not only are our social and professional identities on-line, but also enable huge reach of connectivity putting in to practice the old dictum **'it is not about what you know, but who you know'**.

On the other hand there is a need in parallel for much smaller, exclusive networks that live to a different dictum, namely **'it is not just about who you know, but how willing they are to help.'**

The size of your network clearly matters and will always matter. But being in addition part of a small, intimate group or alumni network, will provide extra significant value.

Leveraging the Power of Instagram

I consider myself an expert user of LinkedIn. I also regularly use Facebook and Twitter.

However when it comes to Instagram, I must confess to being a little ignorant.

So I approached the one super user of Instagram that I know, my 13 year old daughter Dalia.

Dalia has 4000+ followers (and growing) and kindly agreed to give me a 101 on Instagram to help me figure out why and how schools should use it.

Let's start with the basics.

Instagram is an app that allows you to quickly and easily build professional looking photos (and videos) and share them on existing social networks like Facebook, Twitter, Tumblr and Flickr.

Furthermore Graduway's own research shows that Instagram is the fastest growing social network being adopted by education institutions today.

So two obvious questions: does your school need to even be on Instagram, and if yes, what exactly should you be doing?

Let me start by sharing three stats which I believe will persuade you that every school needs to seriously consider using Instagram.

1. As of January 2016, we know **400+ million people** are actively using Instagram each month,

making it one of those social networks just on sheer size that you cannot ignore.

2. According to Wikipedia, 90% of these users are **under the age of 35.**

3. Finally it has been shown by Marketing Charts that with respect to the education demographic, users with some college education proved to be the **most active users** on Instagram.("The Demographics of Instagram and Snapchat Users", *Marketing Charts,* October 29, 2013.)

So if you are interested in engaging alumni, especially younger alumni using social media, you probably need to be doing something on Instagram. But what exactly?

I found an interesting case study by looking at what the Simon Fraser University (SFU) is doing with their alumni on Instagram. SFU launched their official Instagram account in

March 2015 (you can follow **@sfualumni_** or go to **instagram.com/sfualumni_).**

SFU's stated goal is to have "a fantastic way to give our followers an insight into the life of the University even after graduation, whether it is through photos of campus across the seasons or photos of special events in the University, as well as news and updates of SFU alumni exclusive privileges and events."

And so far they have been reasonably successful. They have 740 followers with 206 posts. Moreover they have also effectively launched a popular hashtag within Instagram by inviting SFU alumni and students to join and show their love for the university by taking a picture and tagging it with **#SFUAlumniPride.** This alone has already generated 370 posts.

SFU is doing good work in this area and is probably ahead of the game versus other schools. However there does seem to be a deeper question here regarding social media in general and Instagram in particular. What is it that a school is actually trying to achieve with their social media? Does generating extra alumni followers, likes or posts translate into helping achieve the strategic goals of the school?

I believe there are two common problems with schools' social media strategies.

Firstly I believe many schools simply treat their social media - be it Facebook, Twitter or Instagram - as an alternative to email.

Schools tend to use social media as an alumni communication tool rather than an engagement tool.

This one dimensional approach misses both the opportunity to have a conversation *with the alum individually* but also of facilitating conversations *between alumni*.

Secondly I believe many schools are failing to think about the value proposition to the alum in their social media strategy. Yes you have a captive audience, but what are you sharing with them and will it be considered valuable by them or not?

I don't have all the answers but I believe these are the right first questions. We need to be using Instagram with our alumni but avoiding the old mistakes we typically commit when using social media. Instagram has the potential to unleash huge engagement with our alumni, it's now up to us to be creative in unlocking that value.

Don't Wish Me Happy Birthday

It's my birthday. 39 years old today.

And who remembered that it's my
birthday? Well a curious group of people.

My wife and children woke me up with a chorus
of happy birthdays traditionally sang off-key
and a little too loud.

A few friends on Facebook posted their best
wishes on my timeline.

Fourteen people on LinkedIn wrote me best
wishes messages - two of which I had to look up
their profiles to ascertain who exactly they were
and how we were connected.

I then got three messages from random contacts
on Skype.

I got a 'heart-felt' text message from my pension fund wishing me well.

I got an email from my car insurance company sending me their best wishes and also reminding me of my forthcoming renewal date.

I got only one, yes just one physical card from my older sister.

Finally, my parents left me a voicemail message.

Now I know I sound very grumpy, which is not my intent. I am grateful that people took the time to reach out to me on my special day. The problem is that the day feels less special than it used to.

My birthday experience seems to be a microcosm of our modern lives.

On the one hand we are super connected to a very broad range of people who all have access to us in real time.

On the other hand we have lost the intimacy of relationships. I am less able to differentiate between myself and the various individuals and groups in my life. All seem to merge into one huge social network.

I love the fact that I am connected to 1 billion people on Facebook, but how willing are those people to actually help me?

The future will be about returning intimacy to our relationships; about being able to reintroduce words like 'special', 'best' and 'exclusive' into our on-line networking and communication.

The future will continue to be about being very broadly connected, but also about having deeper connectivity as well.

The future will have a new networking maxim. It will not be just about who you know, but how willing they are to help you.

There is a significant opportunity for education institutions in particular to take advantage of their ability to cut through the 'noise' of our super connected world.

Any institution that can provide access to an exclusive network that is willing to help, while leveraging modern social networks, has a huge value proposition to offer its alumni and members.

The future is about to get smaller, more intimate, more exclusive, and ironically as a result, more deeply connected.

Can You Answer 2 'LinkedIn Group' Questions?

There are over 2 million LinkedIn groups.

It seems that every education institution in the world now has its own official LinkedIn group.

I speak to many schools on a weekly basis and normally two questions come up in conversation - one of which they know the answer to, and the other which they usually don't.

The first question is 'How Big is your LinkedIn Group?'

Every institution will know roughly the size of its LinkedIn group. That number is usually a large one and a source of great pride for the school, and rightly so. It is very positive that so many alumni have voluntarily and proactively attached themselves in such a public way to their alma mater.

The second question that many cannot answer is 'How Engaged is your LinkedIn Group?'

It is troubling to think that many schools do not know the engagement levels of their Group, especially considering that LinkedIn has kindly made this data available to all. In fact, you can view the engagement statistics for all 2 million groups so that you can know not just the engagement for your own school, but compare versus others as well.

I have taken the liberty of creating a 30 second explanatory video to help schools quickly find the engagement statistics for any LinkedIn

Group. Please click on the following link: http://screencast.com/t/q7s3ZGFD

I am a big believer that the first step in improving on-line engagement is to measure and understand your current performance. The data is easily available.

I hope this video can help your school.

The New LinkedIn University Rankings

You may have not seen it yet but LinkedIn deserves a big thank you from all of us for publishing its new University Rankings last week. This is part of a series of excellent tools by LinkedIn for Universities.

The LinkedIn University Rankings is based on **career outcomes** by firstly identifying the top companies for a specific career, then looking at which school the people who work at these companies graduated from, and finally comparing the percentage of alumni of a school who have landed these jobs.

The publishing of this ranking coincides with two trends that I have been posting about in recent weeks.

On the one hand prospective students are looking for school rankings that is broader than just return on investment and needs to include softer factors such as location, flexibility, gender mix, and alumni networking.

On the other hand it is probably true that the most important criteria remains the financial return from their education and the entering into a career of their choice. This is reflected in overt marketing by some schools to highlight their 'career outcomes' credentials as I posted recently about in the case of the University of Phoenix.

So if you are looking for a ranking that is purely focused on return on investment, then LinkedIn University Rankings could potentially be very powerful as its sample size is significantly bigger than any other ranking - rather than surveying just a few thousand alumni, LinkedIn is able to leverage the profile data of millions of alumni. Moreover rather than relying on the accuracy of reported salary increases as other surveys do, the LinkedIn University Rankings focuses on the actual 'career outcome' of which profession you are in.

The only caveat to this ranking is identifying which is really the 'cause' and which is the 'effect' in the career outcome. However this is no different to other rankings.

Overall, this is a big step forward in helping provide students with transparency as to which school will really help them in their chosen career path. Well done LinkedIn.

Image taken from Aston University website.

Chapter 5 – Thinking Out of the Box

Rethinking Alumni Relations for Seniors

The world of education is facing a number of demographic changes.

I recently wrote about the growth of alumni from emerging markets such as China and the opportunity this presents to schools.
However there is another demographic change that offers a different but
significant opportunity to alumni relations professionals.

Students appear to be getting older, but are alumni relations departments changing their approach in response?

A recent article in the New York Times highlighted the change some leading education institutions like Tulane University are making to respond to this growth in adult learners by creating a program to help alumni focus on second careers with a social purpose. Moreover the prize of attracting mature students means that alumni relations with specifically older alumni is becoming more important. As Art Koff, founder of the website RetiredBrains.com, quoted in the same New York Times article explained

Campus classes are a natural pull for loyal alumni. If I were advising universities on ways to increase revenue, I would target boomers, seniors and retirees, particularly alumni, with information on being able to audit certain classes and then try to convert them to pay for additional courses.

Furthermore, executive education programs are yet another clear example of the significant value that comes from treating alumni as potential repeat customers.

So what does this mean for alumni relations departments?

Well for a long-time, colleagues in development functions have been aware that older alumni are an important segment. However this segment also offers schools a unique alumni relations opportunity.

Normally with alumni engagement the focus is about the unique value proposition that your school offers alumni.

For older alumni this would mean providing professional and social value but ensuring that it is relevant to their life-stage.

However what is also different with this segment is that the engagement is based less upon what they can *get* from the alumni network, but much more about what they can *give back*.

Examples include giving senior alumni the chance to share their accumulated wisdom through becoming a mentor, a role model, or providing guest lectures.

What do you think senior alumni need that their school can uniquely assist with?

Wasting the Chinese Alumni Opportunity

The number of international students continues to grow each year.

Yet for most schools, their approach to alumni relations has remained the same.

It feels like education institutions do not give sufficient attention to their alumni from outside their home country.

This seems like a wasted opportunity.

According to an article in Bloomberg citing a report by the Institute of International Education (IIE), the number of Chinese students at U.S. universities jumped 75 percent in three years, reaching almost 275,000 in the last academic year.

Students from China made up the largest contingent among the 886,052 foreign students last year, with 31 percent. India is second with 12 percent of the total, followed by South Korea with 7.7 percent.

Today international students represent about 4.2 percent of total enrollments at U.S. institutions.

But I suppose the real question is how high does the enrollment for international students have to rise before schools change their approach to international alumni relations?

Alumni 'Round the World

Imagine if you were a prospective student from China, considering in which school to enroll.

Wouldn't a critical factor be the school that best provided an alumni 'career community' back in China for you to join after graduation?

Wouldn't you be looking for a school to provide a network of mentors, placements, introductions and jobs that you could benefit from back in your <u>home</u> country?

144

The schools that will win the race for international student enrollment will be those that can provide a strong career offering to their alumni, critically back in the <u>home</u> country of those alumni.

Three basic first steps:

1. Do you provide international students and alumni with their own network?

2. Is that network easy to use in terms of being in the local language and integrated with local social networks?

3. Do you sufficiently leverage your international alumni to help recruit and select new students from their home country?

The international alumni opportunity, and particularly the Chinese one, is growing.

It's time to make a change in how we do international alumni relations.

What if President Obama Was Your Alum?

A hypothetical question - what would your school do if it had a really famous alum like President Obama?

According to Wikipedia, no less than eight education institutions claim President Obama as their alum (St. Francis of Assisi Catholic School, Besuki School, Calvert School, Punahou School, Occidental College, Columbia College, Harvard Law School and he also taught at the University of Chicago Law School).

It is great that each of these institutions is proud to name President Obama as their alum, but beyond bragging rights, does this have any other significance?

In fact, go to virtually any alumni website of any school and they all have a page listing their most famous alumni.

The real question is so what?

Does anyone really care that a school has a famous alum unless it can show a direct and significant causal relationship between the school and the career outcome of that alum?

In the case of President Obama, many are quick to quote Colombia and Harvard Law School when attributing his academic background to particular institutions, but were they his biggest influences? After all it was actually at Occidental College in February 1981, where President Obama made his first public speech. He called for Occidental to participate in the disinvestment from South Africa in response to that nation's policy of apartheid. As such, one could make an argument that Occidental had the biggest impact on his eventual career outcome!

To demonstrate my point further, Harvard claims no less than seven US Presidents as alumni (John Adams, John Quincy Adams, Theodore Roosevelt, Franklin Roosevelt, John F. Kennedy, George W. Bush and Barack Obama). Is there something special about the

Harvard experience that produces American presidents or is it simply people with the potential to be president happen to go to Harvard?

The cause and effect of the career outcome of the alum is the critical ingredient and is often the one neglected by schools.

So what do schools need to do to leverage their alumni beyond bragging rights?

Firstly, with famous alumni, schools need to highlight not just their fame but their direct involvement in their career outcome. This can be as simple as interviewing famous alumni and getting them to explain the impact of their time at your institution in achieving their career goals.

Secondly, schools in general need to deprioritize their famous alumni. Famous alumni will always represent a tiny proportion of the student body.

What is more relevant is to focus on the successful career outcomes of 'regular alumni'.

This is not hard to do. LinkedIn is a fabulous tool in providing data for every school on the career outcomes not just of famous alumni, but more importantly of *regular alumni.*

It is right that schools want to showcase their alumni. However the success stories that will attract future students are not about how many Presidents you have 'created', but how many relevant regular professionals you have produced. Moreover it will critically be about getting those regular alumni to provide testimonials as to the cause and effect of attending your institution on their career outcome.

So let's imagine **not** that President Obama was your alum. But rather let's imagine what you could do with an army of success stories from regular alumni providing inspiration to prospective students and mentoring your graduating students.
This seems to me to be way more powerful than a celebrity alumni headline.

Do you agree that schools fail to adequately explain the cause and effect of the career outcomes of their alumni?

How has your school demonstrated success stories of regular alumni to prospective students?

Which would you rather have, a few famous alumni or a mass of success stories from regular alumni?

Expert Alumni Advice for the New Year

A new year, a new chance for everyone working in the world of education to take their alumni interactions up a level or two. But where to start?

Well, a good place to start is to learn and reapply best practice from other leading institutions.

I recently heard a fascinating expert panel discussion on global best practice in alumni relations and advancement at the Graduway Global Leaders Summit, held at the Said Business School, Oxford University.

What emerged from the discussion was not just what best practice looks like today, but critically what are the key questions every institution should be asking and trying to address.

The panel was chaired by Chris Marshall, Vice President at Grenzebach Glier and Associates, and included a panel of distinguished experts and global thought leaders including:

- Elizabeth Crabtree, Assistant Vice President for Strategy and Resource Development, Brown University
- Jane Szele, Director of Alumni Relations, Saïd Business School
- Rod Lohin, Executive Director, Rotman Alumni Network, Rotman School of Management
- Michael Osbaldeston OBE, Director of Quality Services, EFMD
- Raphaëlle Gautier, Marketing and Development Director, HEC Paris
Click on the video below to see the full recording of the panel discussion.

I have taken the liberty of summarizing what I think were five of the most important trends / best practices that came out from the discussion so that you can benchmark your own school's progress.

1. **Fund-raising vs Friend-raising** - the borders between alumni relations, development and communication are fast fading as schools take a more integrated approach to their alumni. *How integrated is your school's approach to your alumni?*

2. **Measuring and tracking engagement** - if schools are going to be successful in advancement, then they need to at least capture and measure data on their key performance indicators. This would probably be not just donations, but would also include broader engagement metrics such as event attendance, surveys of goodwill towards your institution and volunteering metrics. *Has your school defined its key engagement metrics and tracks and measures them consistently?*

3. **Global vs local approach** - schools need to determine based upon their scale, strategy, and alumni concentrations the best approach to engaging

alumni and whether a global or local/chapter approach makes more sense. *Has your school aligned on the best approach to meeting the local needs of your alumni wherever in the world they are based?*

4. **Culture of engagement** - successful institutions are building today, while students are still on campus, the alumni culture that they would like for the future. *Is your school making steps today towards building a long term culture of loyalty and engagement with alumni?*

5. **Alumni affinity** - schools are now looking at new ways to engage alumni by broadening traditional affinities beyond class groupings to include in particular more career and professionally relevant affinities. *Has your school started to provide an offering to alumni that addresses their career and professional affinities?*

The panel discussion raised intriguing questions for virtually every school, irrespective of their size, location or level of sophistication, on what best practice looks like by beginning to ask the right questions.

What did you learn from the discussion? Do you agree that these are the critical questions that need to be asked? Did our experts miss anything?

What are the key trends that you see and are looking to apply and turn into best practice in 2016?

Alumni Relations in 2020. Are You Ready?

I had the privilege of hearing an insightful panel discussion on the future of alumni relations at the Graduway Global Leaders Summit, held at the Said Business School, Oxford University.
The panel was chaired by Rob Curtis, Vice President of Graduway and focused on the biggest trends and themes affecting the future world of alumni relations.
The distinguished panel included:

- Charles Hardy, Higher Education Evangelist at LinkedIn

- James Stofan, Vice President, Alumni Relations at Tulane University

- Christine Fairchild, Director of Alumni Relations at Oxford University

- Daniel Porter-Jones, Alumni Relations and Development Manager, University of South Wales

- Dan Keyworth, Head of Customer Engagement, Blackbaud

- Della Bradshaw, Business Education Editor, Financial Times

Please see below the panel discussion in full.

Probably for the first time in one of my blogs, I am not going to propose any answers and instead will leave that for the experts in this panel.

I do however believe that when talking about the future, most of the value is derived from asking the right questions.

What are the major questions facing both education and corporate institutions in planning their future alumni relations? I would suggest the following:

- **Emerging markets:-** what is the impact from the change in size and mix of alumni towards emerging markets like China?
- **Big data:-** which data do institutions need to have in the future that they do not capture today?
- **MOOCs** - what challenges and opportunities does this provide to the world of alumni relations?
- **Career outcomes** - given LinkedIn and the Financial Times' focus on career outcomes in their school rankings, how important will alumni relations be when compiling school rankings in the future?
- **Skills** - which skills and knowledge will we need to be developing, training and recruiting in our alumni relations teams to deal with the alumni relations of the future?
- **Value** - what is the unique value proposition that your institution is going to provide its alumni? (See

my blog on my interview with Sean Brown from McKinsey)

- **Culture** - how are you going to build the right culture of giving and engagement now that will bear fruit in the future? (See my blog on the keynote by Elise Betz from Pennsylvania University)

The world of education and in particular its alumni relations is at a number of exciting cross roads.

What do you think are the most important trends affecting alumni relations?

Which are the biggest threats and opportunities facing your institution in how it does alumni relations?

What questions are you asking about alumni relations in 2020?

Insights from McKinsey's Alumni Relations Program

I had the privilege of interviewing three weeks ago Sean Brown at the Graduway Global Leaders Summit, held at the Said Business School, Oxford University. During our talk "From the Boardroom to the Classroom" Sean shared a unique perspective based on over 10 years' experience running leading corporate and academic alumni networks.

Sean is currently the Global Director of Alumni Relations at McKinsey & Company, Inc., where for the past seven years he has led the management consultancy's program to engage and strengthen its network of nearly 30,000 former consultants in over 100 countries around the world. Prior to McKinsey, Sean served as the Global Director of Alumni Relations at the Massachusetts Institute of Technology Sloan School of Management.

Please see below my interview in full with Sean.

There were a number of amazing insights that Sean shared in the interview, but I want to focus here on just three critical things that I took away as relevant for anyone looking to build and develop a professional network, be it a corporate or an academic institution.

1. **Offer a unique value proposition**- McKinsey do this by providing their alumni with access to a) an exclusive network via their official directory where all alumni irrespective of their seniority are easily available to one another, b) career opportunities and top talent for recruitment which strengthens engagement and builds the network and finally c) ongoing access to the firm's latest thinking via twice monthly global knowledge sessions with cutting edge content for their alumni. I believe most academic institutions and corporations could provide a similar value proposition if they were focused on

this as a goal and prepared to work collaboratively across departments.

2. **Provide a secure environment**- McKinsey have invested in offering a secure platform and the ongoing authentication of their alumni, which is critical in providing a trusted environment for networking.

3. **Create a culture of engagement** -Probably the most critical ingredient. McKinsey has created a 'pay it forward' culture which everyone is exposed to from day one. In fact Sean's explanation of how McKinsey embeds this engagement culture from the moment consultants join the firm echoed what I shared previously from University of Pennsylvania's Elise Betz on how to build a culture of philanthropy and engagement.

It was truly inspiring to hear Sean describe McKinsey's 'joined-up' approach to their alumni relations. I believe that there is a significant opportunity for both academic institutions and corporations to also apply these best practices, particularly in building that elusive engagement culture.

What do you think are the most important learnings from McKinsey's approach to alumni relations?

Do you agree that every institution has the potential to create a strong engagement culture?

Which is the biggest barrier in applying this approach to your organization?

What Can P&G Teach Us About Alumni Relations?

I left Procter & Gamble almost a decade ago, but the two basic rules of branding have stayed with me ever since. Firstly, the need to segment your consumers. Secondly, to provide a differentiated value proposition based upon that segmentation.

It is hard to imagine given my receding hairline, but I worked in the sexy world of haircare with some of the world's great shampoo brands like Pantene, Head & Shoulders, Herbal Essences, Vidal Sassoon and Wash & Go. Each targeted a different type of shampoo consumer, based upon criteria such as age, gender and time spent on haircare products. Can you imagine what would have happened if P&G had offered just one brand to meet the needs of all its different consumers?

So what does this have to do with the world of education?

Well, it often feels that schools treat all their alumni as if they were the same. Taking P&G's example, it should not be that way.

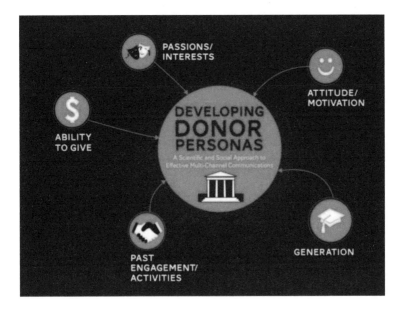

I also want to differentiate here between segmentation for fundraising, and segmentation for alumni relations.

For fundraising I think many schools do a very good job in segmenting their donors. See a great presentation as an example by Becky Vardaman, Vice President of Strategy at Converge Consulting, who provided a useful approach at the CASE V and VI Presentation on Alumni Segmentation presentation. As we also heard this week at the Global Leaders Summit, some leaders, like Elizabeth Crabtree from Brown University, have developed some very innovative criteria for fundraising. For example, if alumni are married to one another it is a much stronger indicator of higher giving. However when it comes to segmenting alumni relations, it feels like schools do less well. Many schools assume that one value proposition should fit the needs of all their alumni.

For alumni relations, should schools not be differentiating their communications, and critically, what they offer to alumni based upon criteria like age, gender, sexual orientation, race, religion, as well as more obvious ones such as location, industry and seniority?

Each school will of course need to develop its own alumni segmentation based upon its unique background, culture and history, and which segments are more meaningful and addressable for their institution. Moreover the segmentation if done correctly, should lead to a specific offering that will make the alumni network more relevant for its members.

It's 2016 and alumni simply expect more. They expect at the very least that their alma mater has made a first attempt at making their relationship more personal and relevant for them.

Do you think schools are segmenting their approach to alumni relations with the same rigor that they do for fundraising?

Which is the most important basis to segment your alumni? How feasible is it to provide different offering to different alumni?

Do you have some success stories of implementing an alumni segmentation?

Higher Education Is Not Ready to Be Disrupted

I hear it all the time. So probably do you. Higher education is ripe for disruption.

I have seen the worried looks of deans and vice-chancellors at conference after conference, many at a loss as how best to compete with the MOOCs (Massive Open Online Courses) threat posed by Coursera, edX and others.

I won't rehearse the arguments of why higher education is ripe for disruption - you can see well written articles in both Forbes and The Economist for that.

And you know what, higher education may well be ripe for disruption but it will not happen any time soon.

Let me suggest why.

Yes, 10 million people and growing have signed up for Coursera on-line courses, but that still cannot be defined as disruption. How many people do you know who have decided not to go to college, and are instead going to do a series of MOOCs? How likely will it be that this will happen anytime soon?

For disruption in any industry to work, there needs to be an overwhelming motivation from either the buyer or supplier on why the new way of doing things makes huge sense.

On paper, the payers for higher education have a huge incentive for a 'free' model. Who wouldn't want to use their 'college fund' of thousands of dollars for something else?

Yet however good a MOOC is, it will not yet replace the market incumbent – the college higher education system that has remained virtually untouched for decades.

The market incumbent, has three strong advantages vs a MOOC, and one knock-out advantage.

1. **Campus experience** – can a MOOC get close to offering the memories and personal growth that comes from a campus experience?
2. **Face to face teaching** – there remains a significant difference between face to face teaching and virtual teaching although I concede the gap has narrowed.
3. **Access to an exclusive alumni network** – can a MOOC offer you access to an alumni network as exclusive and as willing to help?

Schools are rightly trying to differentiate themselves from MOOCs by highlighting and improving their offering in these three areas.

However even if MOOCs could compete in these three areas, they are still missing the key disruptive ingredient for higher education.

Are employers willing to change the fundamental selection process of how they hire?

Disruption in higher education will only come when recruitment managers in companies are willing to recruit graduates of a MOOC as equals to those from a college.

The recruitment managers not only need to be convinced that the educative experience of MOOCs has equally prepared applicants for their companies, but in addition they have to overcome their own emotional bias of agreeing to commoditize their own higher education that they themselves spent thousands of dollars on.

In the western higher education system, MOOCs at best seem destined to play perhaps a limited 'blended' role. Schools will offer a MOOC as a clever marketing 'sample' initiative to provide potential students with a taster of what they can offer or maybe for standard popular courses.

If disruption ever comes it will start with lower ranked schools in the developed world, and in general in the developing world where the 'free' option seems more attractive, and the hiring classes are less likely to be biased in favor of a college education.

Higher education institutions may want to consider offering MOOCs as part of a 'freemium' model. However they may well be better off investing in improving the campus experience, the quality of teaching and the access and exclusivity of their alumni network.

These are the things that build their brand and better protect them from the commoditization of MOOCs should it ever come.

Do you think higher education will be disrupted, and if so, when?

Is there a difference between the developed and emerging markets? Between elite, mid-tier and bottom tier schools?

Would you ever give parity to someone who had completed some MOOCs with someone who has a college education?

Probably the Best University in the World

Let's imagine together what the best university in the world could look like.

Its lectures would be given by TED.

Its campus would be run by Google.

Its research would be by Nobel Prize Winners.

Its admission policy would be a pure meritocracy with the best students chosen from around the world.

Its alumni network would be run by McKinsey.

Its tuition fees would be zero.

Its education would be continuous and for life.

Picking the right benchmark is half the battle in achieving greatness in education.

Are these the right benchmarks? How does your education institution stack up?

The 50 Most Powerful Alumni Networks - Really?

I saw an interesting post last week from my respected colleague Andy Shaindlin that got me thinking.

Andy's blog How Not to Rank Alumni Networks? gave a critique of the ranking of alumni networks provided by The Economist. In fact it turns out there are lots of rankings of alumni networks out there.

For example Best Colleges provides a ranking of the top 50 most powerful college alumni networks. Their analysis considers financial contributions from alumni, employment rates, student ratings and the reputation of the school. Despite the apparent robustness of their approach, the result was a bit of an anti-climax.

Drumroll...

In third place - Columbia.

In second place - Harvard.

In first place - Stanford.

Now, who could have possibly guessed at such an outcome?

I suppose my disappointment is that all the analyses out there are self-fulfilling.

If you are going to include factors like financial contributions or reputation then it is not surprising if the biggest institutions come out on top?

This means at the end of the analysis we have a ranking that is of no practical help to anyone.

I also think these rankings fundamentally misunderstand what 'power' really means when it comes to alumni networking.

I think there are two critical factors that I look at when assessing alumni network power:

1. **Willingness to help** - how willing is your alumni network to help you as an individual? An alumni network is only as powerful as its accessibility and the willingness of that network to help one another.

2. **Relative power** - absolute power is also less interesting that value. How much have you as an individual had to invest (both money and time) to be part of that network and to benefit from its power? I am looking to build a comprehensive alumni networking ranking that would provide fairer and more valuable insights.

Please let me have your feedback as to what to include.

Is alumni networking power a relative or absolute measure?

What are the critical factors that you think should be included?

How would you use such a ranking to help your school?

Which is the Most Powerful Network - McKinsey, LinkedIn or Harvard Business School?

Ask an average person in the street, which is the most powerful professional network in the world and I suggest they will reply with one of the three following answers: McKinsey, LinkedIn or Harvard Business School.

They are each a leading professional network of their type - corporate, social and academic. Yet what is it that makes each of these networks so powerful? And more importantly, can their respective sources of power be used and emulated by other networks? Let's look at each one in turn.

1. McKinsey & Company

In some respects the above picture of three McKinsey alumni, as published in the Financial Times, says it all. The McKinsey alumni network is quite simply the most prestigious professional network in the world as an article by Duff

McDonald points out. Given its size of just over 30,000 people,

It is extraordinary that so many alumni are in senior leadership positions around the world including 150 who are CEOs of companies with revenues exceeding $1 billion.

Moreover McKinsey has a reputation of providing a network for life that actively facilitates the careers of its members both inside and outside of the firm. In short McKinsey's network power is based on its culture and ability to provide members with access to the world's 'movers and shakers'.

MILLION MEMBERS

We now have 300 million LinkedIn members, more than half of whom live outside of the U.S. That's enough to make LinkedIn the fourth largest country in the world. In celebration, we took a look back to see how much our membership has grown and diversified over the past five years. It's a helpful reminder of not only where we've been, but also where we're headed as we work to create economic opportunity for every professional in the world.

2. LinkedIn

LinkedIn is the world's largest professional network with 330 million people and growing. LinkedIn's huge networking power is based upon its size and how easy it has made it for people to reach out to almost anyone they need to meet.

To get an idea of its sheer size, if LinkedIn was a country - it would now be the 3rd biggest country by population in the world - ahead of the United States and behind just China and India.

It has revolutionized the old networking world dictum of 'it's not what you know but who you know' and connected people professionally like no one else before it. Could you now even contemplate professional networking without LinkedIn?

3. Harvard Business School

And last but not least, Harvard Business School. Your alma mater, even if not HBS, probably has something special with which to compete. Its alumni network as opposed to most corporate and social networks, (McKinsey potentially an exception) is built with a significant ingredient of emotional commitment. As such, a school's alumni network is often based on a different dictum to the previous two networks.

A school's alumni network dictum is 'not just who you know, but crucially how willing they are to help'.

I believe this power comes from the fact that it's not just an exclusive professional network but also a social one. Don't we all strive to help friends and family in life first?

So three powerful networks, but each with a slightly different source to that power.

Clearly for most organizations, be it a school or a corporation, the interesting question is not simply which is the most powerful network of the three, but how can we incorporate what is amazing about each of these three networks into our own networks?

There seems to be similar themes emerging that we can all try and apply to our own professional networks:

The need for an exclusive and trusted brand, the need for a clear professional value proposition, the ease and ability to provide access to the right people, and finally the need for an emotional commitment and willingness to help one another.

I would welcome your thoughts.

Which do you think is the most powerful professional network today?

Can all organizations really incorporate and replicate some of the strength of these networks?

What in your opinion is the real source of power of professional networks?

Which is the Bigger Brand - Harvard or Apple?

Ask an average person in the street to name the biggest brand in the world? They will probably answer Apple. But is that necessarily true?

Well Forbes would agree that Apple is the biggest brand in the world based on earnings. It published its 'world's most valuable brands' ranking which assesses more than 200 global brands. Forbes does this by taking their estimated contribution to earnings of each brand and applying an average price/earnings ratio. The table below shows the top five biggest earning brands according to Forbes with Apple heading the list.

Rank ▲	Brand	Brand Value ($bil)	1-Yr Value Change (%)	Brand Revenue ($bil)	Company Advertising ($mil)	Industry
1	Apple	104.3	20	156.5	1,100	Technology
2	Microsoft	56.7	4	77.8	2,600	Technology
3	Coca-Cola	54.9	9	23.5	3,342	Beverages
4	IBM	50.7	5	104.5	1,339	Technology
5	Google	47.3	26	43.5	772	Technology

However Forbes may be missing something.

The value of a brand in the 'for-profit' world is normally generated through its product's look, feel and usefulness and hence the earnings it generates. Yet a ranking methodology based only on earnings will of course neglect other important brand attributes. This is particularly true for brands found in the 'not-for-profit' sector.

Let's take the education sector as an example where schools have very valuable brands. If we changed the ranking criteria away from just earnings, and broadened it to include attributes like 'trust', 'exclusivity', 'desirability' and 'loyalty', then we may well get a few surprises. I imagine we would see some of the world's great higher education brands challenging for the top spots of the rankings.

Do people trust Apple more than they trust their old school?

Is Microsoft a more exclusive brand than their alma mater?

Is IBM really a more desirable brand than their college?

Moreover - on the critical attribute of loyalty - I often see people wearing clothing with branding from their college like Harvard, UCLA, Brown - can you say the same for any of these great corporations? Corporations arguably do not come close to attaining the emotional brand connection that the non-profit sector generates.

So let's move the debate on a little.

Let's agree that many schools have valuable brands against which the for-profit world would place significant value. So maybe the right question to ask is if schools are sitting on brands that are worth potentially billions of dollars, are they leveraging the full potential of that brand power?

I suggest the answer is 'no'. On a micro level, I see in my daily interactions with higher education and K12 schools, many that have the opportunity to leverage their brand more aggressively in their offering to both students and alumni. This can be about improving donations and making the environment for their alumni a more trusted experience and exclusive offers leading to higher engagement. However I believe it can be much more than this.

On a macro level, I think there is a significant opportunity for school brands to take a greater leadership role, alongside these highly ranked corporations, in shaping global thinking and making the world a better place.

I would welcome your thoughts. Can non-profit brands challenge the supremacy of corporate brands? Which is the biggest brand in the world? What should schools be doing to realize the full potential of their brands?

Turning the Tables - Ranking School Rankings

If you are in a senior position in a school, probably nothing is more terrifying than the publication of the latest school ranking.

I thought it would be interesting to turn the tables (pardon the pun) and do a ranking of 'school rankings', with this post focused on business school rankings.

There are a number of publications that regularly rank business schools - the Financial Times, US News, Forbes and Economist to name a few. Each publication has its own methodology but which is the most reliable?

Well probably the best place to start would be to ask recent customers of business schools - namely alumni - and let them decide which are the most important criteria for ranking a school.

In August 2013, Graduway conducted its Business School Graduation Survey where 1,081 recent graduates from business schools in US, UK, Canada and Australia were asked which factors influenced most their choice of school and then to grade their school on how well they performed against these factors in reality.

The results gave us an indication as to the best criteria, in a perfect world, to evaluate and rank schools against.

The table below compares the weighting of each criteria that the alumni in our survey suggested, with the weighting used by major publications. To provide a simpler comparison, I have aggregated all the criteria into four major criteria as shown below. Please be aware this is not an exact science and is based upon my reading of their published methodologies.

	Graduway Survey	Financial Times	US News	Forbes	Economist
Salary and ROI	36%	45%	14%	100%	20%
Network and career	20%	7%	21%	0%	45%
Quality of faculty/students	13%	20%	65%	0%	35%
Soft (location, flexibility, gender)	31%	28%	0%	0%	0%
Total	100%	100%	100%	100%	100%

Without delving into all the numbers here, there seem to be a number of directional conclusions:

1. Most rankings over emphasize salary increases. Nearly all the rankings seem to place too much emphasis on salary increases and return on investment. In any case salary criteria often have an inherent bias in favor of schools in certain countries (the US for example) whose employment markets give bigger premiums for recently qualified MBAs.

2. Yes to career placement, but what about alumni networks? The detailed data shows that although schools do a reasonable job on career and placement opportunities, they are under-performing on alumni networking.

3. Quality of the faculty is not as important for alumni. Nearly all the rankings over emphasize the importance of the quality of the faculty versus the value attributed by alumni.

4. Don't forget 'softer' factors. With the exception of the Financial Times, most publications do not seem to explicitly cover or give sufficient weighting to factors like flexibility, the desired location of the institution, gender balance and the ability to make their education broadening from an international / global perspective.

In conclusion, this is not an exact science when it comes to ranking and the data is not perfect. However it feels that all the publications need to adjust their rankings if possible to be a little more balanced especially on those softer factors and alumni networking.

And finally, if you forced me to choose between the rankings...........I think based on this data that the Financial Times is probably the ranking that comes closest to what alumni have told us they want from their school.

I would welcome your feedback and be happy to share the more detailed data with interested parties. I would particularly be interested in hearing which criteria you would like to see have greater weighting in future school rankings.

Chapter 6 – Avoiding Classic Mistakes

5 Big Mentoring Mistakes

A few weeks ago I wrote a blog called The Case for Mentoring.

There, I highlighted the latest research by Gallup-Purdue University which showed that the key to students achieving long term success *after* college was having a mentor *during* college.

If like me, you are convinced that all our students need a mentor, what is the best way to make this happen?

The answer lies in using a combination of both technology (on-line networking platform) and a large group of capable and willing mentors (your army of alumni).

However, too often, I see well-intentioned schools making 5 *big* mistakes. (Please forgive the Julia Roberts clip but I could not resist.)

They are as follows:

1. **Not providing a scalable solution** - manually pairing off students with alumni, one at a time, is not a scalable solution and requires too many resources and man-hours. The goal here is providing *all* students with the opportunity to have a mentor. To do this you must provide an on-line platform where students and alumni can pair themselves off with each other, by the thousands, and without the direct intervention of the school. The school's role here is simply one of facilitation.

2. **Not providing sufficient value for mentors** - usually it is much harder to get mentors (alumni) rather than mentees (students) to join the platform. What is the value proposition to and the motivation for mentors joining your platform? As such, to have a successful mentoring program, you cannot have it as a stand-alone module. It will only work if it is part of a wider alumni networking platform where there are reasons for your mentors to be engaged and

active such as jobs, events, photos, discussions etc. A strong alumni networking platform will lead to a strong mentoring platform within it.

3. **Micro-managing users** - there is a fine balance between facilitating mentoring relationships and *micro-managing* those relationships. Having connected with each other via your platform, your mentors and mentees are quite capable, to organize when, how and where they will communicate going forward. Features such as appointment scheduling, in my opinion, look both clumsy and interfering.

4. **Not making the mentoring specific enough** - providing willing alumni is a good start. However the mentees need to know specifically what each mentor is willing to do and unwilling to do. Mentoring means something different to each of us. The more specific and granular you can make each mentors willingness to help, the more likely the mentoring introductions will actually be successful.

5. **Not making mentoring relevant for your community** - the type of mentoring offered needs to

be specific and relevant to your community. For many this is purely about professional mentoring by finding a mentor in your chosen industry or profession. However for others, it can be social and even spiritual - students finding life coaches and role models that can provide valuable support through their shared gender, sexuality, ethnicity, nationality etc.

Mentoring is a critical offering for all education institutions.

I hope my highlighting these 5 *big* mistakes can improve our chances of doing it right.

Are You Crazy? Don't Build It Yourself. Buy.

So I asked the VP Alumni Relations, why did your institution build its new IT system rather than buy it from an external vendor?

And the answer went something like this...

You are right. It was a mistake. Our IT department is made up of very talented people. And we decided to build it ourselves. But it is not a scratch on what you showing me. In fact I feel sick seeing what you are showing me, knowing that our product will never look as good and we have invested so much time and money.

I can provide some very practical arguments about why it almost never pays for an education institution to build rather than buy their own new IT system, whether it is a new website, database, networking platform or communication tool.

1. **Cost** - it will cost more
2. **Time** - it will take longer
3. **Quality** - it will likely be less good, particularly from the user experience
   Even if one were to make allowances for the fact that your institution has truly unique requirements and customizations, I still do not believe that it would make sense to build.

I have also noticed a strange phenomenon. The larger and wealthier the institution is, the more likely they are to build their own IT systems and to be blunt, the more clunky and outdated their systems look. Wealth in this case seems like a distinct disadvantage.

I have sat with some of the world's best universities in rooms filled with their talented IT people who have the ability to build almost anything.

And here lies the root of the problem. Schools build because they can, not because they should.

The discussion over whether a school should build or buy is overtaken by the simple fact that they have enough internal talent to actually build. But this is not a sufficient reason to do so.

Let me use the crude example of a car. Would you build or buy your own car? For most of us this is a simple decision as we are unable to build, so the only option is to buy. However imagine if you were a very talented engineer, would you really build your own car in your garage or buy one from an experienced automobile company?

Just because you can, is not a sufficient reason to build.

Rather the discussion should be centered around strategic focus. What does your organization do better than anyone else in the world? What is your unique expertise? Where should you be investing your personnel and conversely, where should you be utilizing external experts?

In our fast moving world, I think the discussion is at long last moving decisively in favor of buying because of the emergence of **one new factor, namely access to innovation.**

I was speaking last month to a Vice President of Alumni Affairs at a very prestigious institution. They have very talented IT personnel and budget is simply not an issue. In the past this organization had always built everything internally. Not anymore. This institution has decided to buy its new database from an established industry provider. Their motivation was simple - **it is all about innovation**. Using a database from Blackbaud or Salesforce meant having access to an ecosystem of partner vendors providing in turn access to literally hundreds of innovative products each year.

This was the clear tipping point. Even the biggest university can no longer innovate in this specialized field at the rate of dedicated vendors. If cost, time or quality arguments do not work, then perhaps the final knock-out punch is about having continuous access to cutting edge innovation.

The days of schools building their own systems seem to be over.

Has your organization recently entered into a build versus buy discussion?

What was the deciding factor for you?

What would you recommend as the best way to facilitate such a sensitive internal discussion?

Putting Your Alumni Second

Tough question for you.

You work in Advancement and clearly your alumni are important.

Yet, if there was a choice between making your life easier or your alumni's, which would you choose?

A case in point that I recently came across is 'Single Sign-on.'

'Single Sign-on' is when a school requests that all their alumni sign-on to any of their websites and platforms using one common username and password.

On the face of it this is intended to be 'user-friendly' as surely it is much easier for alumni to sign-on to all of their school systems using just *one* password.

Yet, I would hypothesize that if you asked 100 random alumni to recall their school single sign-on username and password, the majority would struggle to do so.

Moreover there seems to be a much easier alternative available – 'Social Sign-on'. That is asking alumni to sign-on using one of their social networks like Facebook or LinkedIn whose passwords they are much more likely to remember.

So, why do so many schools insist on 'Single Sign-on'? And, is this simple case - an example of a deeper problem?

Simply put, schools seem to put their own needs first, and those of their alumni only second.

Yes, there are lots of advantages for the administrator of a school by using 'Single Sign-on' for easier verification of users and data synchronization. But there are also technical solutions which, with a little more effort and creativity, could deliver the same results, while being easier for alumni.

Truly, it is not always easy to put alumni first. But if we are serious about engaging our alumni then let's start by making it as simple as possible for them to engage with us.

Let's put alumni first.

The Death of Email for Life

For me, 'email for life' is a symbol of how an education institution can become irrelevant to their alumni community.

For those of you who don't already know, 'email for life' is a service that many schools offer their alumni allowing them to continue to use their college email address after graduation.

Let's take a step back for a moment and try to understand what the real value of such a service could be.

For a few weeks or even months after graduation, I could understand why it may be useful for an alum who has not yet found employment to continue using their college email address. But beyond this limited time period, what is the value to alumni of 'email for life'?

Even if you were an alum from a very prestigious institution, when would you actually have the need to use that email address in practice?

I am also assuming that the percentage of alumni who actually regularly use such an address is pretty small.

So if this service is of very limited value to alumni, and probably hardly ever used, why do schools continue to provide it?

My focus here is not specifically about the pros and cons of 'email for life' but more about the underlying issue I think it represents, i.e. *why would schools continue to invest their limited resources into less relevant alumni services?*

Firstly, I think part of the answer is that the old thinking prevails that puts schools at the center of their alumni's world even if the alumni have actually moved on.

Secondly, there is a cultural reluctance to change. The easy option is to simply continue investing resources in the same things year after year.

Finally, I think there is a self-confidence issue. I suspect some alumni professionals do not believe they can actually offer something of value to their alumni so resort to the old ways of doing things.

I fundamentally disagree.

I believe there is a huge opportunity for schools to play a significant and valuable role in the lives of their alumni. This is two-fold:

1. **Career communities** - providing alumni with access to mentors, jobs and connections that can really help them individually and each other.

2. **Life-long learning** - providing alumni with access to both on-going professional development and cutting edge research made available specifically for them. Schools have real potential to be relevant and offer value to their alumni if only they are willing to make that change.

It is time for the 'death' of 'email for life' and all it represents.

It is time for schools to start being relevant again.

Say Goodbye to the Class of 2016. Forever.

The countdown has started.

It is almost March 2016, and for many schools, that means just 12 weeks until graduation.

Time to celebrate? Well not if you are involved in the advancement department of an education institution.

Let me be a little provocative. For what percentage of your alumni will graduation be the last time you ever hear from them again? 30%? 40%? Or worse?

For many of your graduating students the commencement ceremony will be the beginning of a lifetime of zero interaction with your institution.

The big question is why? Why do schools lose touch so quickly?

The technical answer is that the first summer post-graduation will, for many of your alumni, mark big changes in their personal and professional lives.

They will probably start a new role or job. They will probably move location. And of course they will probably have new contact information. Within weeks all of the contact information you hold on these individuals (address, email, phone number) will be out of date.

But that still leaves the underlying question - why? Why do schools lose contact so quickly even if these changes are happening?

The answer is because many schools often only decide to stay in touch with their alumni after they have already left.

In short, schools leave it too late.

In an ideal world, your institution will start to build its culture of philanthropy and alumni engagement not on the last day, but the first day of school.

For those interested in a strategic approach to this, please see Elise Betz, Executive Director of Alumni Relations from the University of Pennsylvania, who recently gave an inspiring keynote speech at the **Graduway Global Leaders Summit.** Her talk, ***"Cultivating Roots: Building a Culture of Student Philanthropy and Engagement",*** was a bold example of how a school (albeit a top one), can strategically invest in their culture of giving with an eye on the very long term.

However what if your school is unable to think that long term and needs a solution in place within the next few weeks?

Here are three tips for you:

1. **Connect via <u>social networks</u>** - get connected with your graduating students via their social networks. Alumni may well change jobs and location but their

Facebook and LinkedIn connection details will stay constant.

2. **Make them part of the alumni network <u>now</u>** - while it is understandable that you only want to reward students with membership of the alumni body once they graduate, it is simply too late. In particular facilitate mentors for them within the wider alumni community.

3. **Give them a reason to stay connected** - show them before they graduate how being part of an exclusive alumni network can help them both professionally and socially.

The clock is ticking. You still have time to save your connection with the Class of 2016, but you need to get moving now.

How Schools Make a Bad First Impression

Most people when asked would agree that first impressions are critical in life.

According to [Forbes you have around 7 seconds](#) to make a favorable first impression. According to [research from the Universities of Glasgow and Princeton](#) it is even quicker with humans making judgements on someone's trustworthiness within the first 500 milliseconds of hearing their voice.

First impressions are also critical in the world of alumni relations.

So imagine you are an alum visiting your school's website or network for the very first time and experience one of the following symptoms:

a) You can see the last post of a discussion or any activity for that matter is more than x months ago.

b) The design and user experience looks like it was cutting edge in 1996.

c) There is zero integration with social networks and little effort made to make things easy for you to use the product.

d) The profiles shown are clearly out of date and have not been updated for a while.

In short the site looks like a **dead network**.

How likely after experiencing such a welcome is it that your alumni will contribute any content or make a return visit in the near future?

The theory of dead networks: the more dead and inactive a site looks, the more dead and inactive it becomes.

Schools are often tempted to combat the symptoms of a dead network by simply adding more and more content. This can be a counter-productive move as the feeling of activity when visiting your site is based not only on the absolute level of user activity, but also in how proportionate it is to the amount of content you have provided. You want to spread whatever level of activity you have over the smallest area possible.

There is some good news however. The theory of dead networks also works in reverse. If a site looks active and engaged, (even if it is not) then this in turn leads to more activity and more engagement.

Some obvious conclusions from the law of dead networks:

Firstly when it comes to content for your alumni, 'less can be more'. Only provide content that is truly exclusive or engaging.

Secondly cut out any 'nice to have' sub groups. You should only allow space for affinity groups or clubs which can generate sufficient activity.

Finally, a school needs to do everything it can from a user experience to make their sites looks fresh, engaged and active and something that it is in constant use. Your site needs to look like it is bursting with activity.

Let the theory of dead networks unleash your school's potential. Activity leads to activity. Make a good first impression and show your alumni that they can be proud members of an active network.

An Alumni Lesson from Ross and Chandler

I recently stumbled across an old 'Friends' episode which is super relevant for anyone running or thinking of running an alumni network.

It's the Friends episode where the characters Ross and Chandler join their respective school's alumni networks for the first time. They then impersonate each other in the network and post inappropriate profile descriptions and updates - even pretending Ross has died, to see how popular he is. I have posted the relatively 'clean' clip below.

The antics of Ross and Chandler tie into a common concern expressed by schools - although they all want to maximize alumni engagement, they are concerned at what alumni will do with this freedom of expression.

What if alumni post inappropriate content about themselves or others in the network?

What if alumni start a discussion that is critical of the school in some way?

What if a recent graduate is too aggressive / familiar in their messaging to an important donor or senior positioned alum?

In short, the flip side of higher alumni engagement could mean some of the risks outlined above, so what is the answer?

Well, the answer is **not** excessive controls where every single comment or posting must be vetted and checked prior to publication. This would kill engagement. The answer is also **not** about restricting free speech.

Yet there are ways to minimize this risk while keeping your network active and engaged:

1. Control access - it sounds basic but an obvious first step is to ensure that only real alumni have access to your network. This includes ensuring all users sign up to your privacy statement and terms and conditions of usage.

2. Student training - your highest risk group may be graduating students. Before inviting this new batch of alumni to join the network, why not provide them with a short training on the 'dos and don'ts' of using the network including how best to approach more experienced alumni.

3. Supporting alumni privacy - each user should have the ability to control their own personal data that is shown about them in the network and to opt out of being messaged if they want. Also provide alumni with options to indicate where they are willing to help other alumni and how best to connect with them so as to guide interactions.

4. Retrospective controls - finally your school must have the ability to remove any offending materials quickly and if necessary to exclude misbehaving users.

My experience of working with many school networks is that in reality alumni can be trusted and misbehavior is very rare / non-existent. Although many schools have a natural fear of giving up some control to make room for alumni engagement, there are ways as outlined to mitigate this risk.

Finally, the best control in a network is 'self-control.' Meaning most of your users will fear being perceived by others in a negative way and hence will control and moderate their own behavior. Remember this is **not** an anonymous network which is probably the greatest control of all.

Trust your alumni! You can encourage alumni engagement while sleeping easy at night.

Be Afraid of Your Customers

I had quite a traumatic week. I woke up Monday morning to a call from my colleague Rob.

Daniel. Have you seen the posting about you on LinkedIn? Someone is publicly asking for you to be banned from the group!

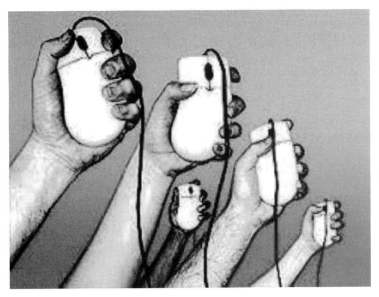

Sure enough he was right. On late Sunday night I had posted my regular blog on one of the key industry LinkedIn groups. Evidently something technical had gone wrong (always happens to me) and my discussion post had now appeared 7 times in a row! A member of the group had seen my 7 postings and assumed it was SPAM and had publicly asked for my removal.

Now the issue for me is that this is a group of thousands of customers and the trending discussion was now about my removal from the group. This is not the type of coverage that is good for business!

As it turns out the person who posted for my removal was very gracious in helping me remove all of the offending materials (both my 7 posts and his one asking for my removal) once I explained the mistake and what had happened.

Yet just as I was calming down by the end of the week, I had yet another traumatic moment.

Someone had started a discussion on a leading industry forum asking if anyone had used my company Graduway before, and what was their feedback. Within 24 hours there were numerous replies - very honest replies! Everything was being discussed in the open for all to see - be it our pricing, quality of service, how well our product worked, what we were like to work with etc. Thankfully the feedback was both fair and positive.

It's a terrifying moment for any business or organization to hear its customers having a group discussion about them. Yet these discussions happen every day. You are not always privy to that discussion, and may at best be a simple observer - praying for your happy customers to speak louder and for your least happy customers to have selective amnesia.

The episode brought into sharp focus how powerful social networks have become. They can literally make or break a reputation in seconds.

What's the solution? You cannot possibly control the conversation about you on social networks. Customers will tell others exactly what they really feel about you.

The only solution is to ensure your product and customer service is always world class and that all your customers, especially your least happy ones, still have something good to say about you.

This also applies to the higher education world. Schools need to ensure that they are delivering for students, parents and especially alumni what they really want. They are our ambassadors for better or for worse.

3 Secrets to a Perfect Campaign

Schools conduct 'campaigns' aimed at their alumni all the time. Yet it may sound obvious but have you ever put yourself in the 'receiving shoes' of those alumni?

Start by collating **all** the various emails and communications that your school has sent in the last few months and put them all together on one virtual table. Is the result a perfectly consistent and coherent message for your alumni? Probably not.

The problem starts with the fact that a school will have many well intentioned staff from different departments (dare I say 'silos') all communicating simultaneously with the same alumni but probably not sufficiently coordinating their campaigns.

Let me describe what this can feel like from an alum's perspective:

Careers is asking them to be a mentor.

Admissions is asking them to be ambassadors.

Alumni Relations is asking them to attend events and volunteer.

Advancement is asking them for money.

While all these requests individually are totally reasonable, requested **simultaneously**, they will lead to the alum being overwhelmed and unclear about what to prioritize. Moreover, build into that picture that each of these departments is probably asking the same alum to login to a separate platform and you begin to feel the alum's confusion.

So what can a school do to better coordinate its campaigns and reduce alumni confusion?

Ten years ago I was working at Procter & Gamble and saw them using very successfully a marketing campaign technique called '**3-H**'

(Hero, Halo, Holistic). '3-H' ensured their marketing campaigns were extremely clear and their consumers' confusion minimized. I think this technique could be applied to alumni campaigns – let me explain.

'3-H' goes like this.

Hero – every 3 months (or more regularly if you prefer) you as a school pick a new campaign from just one department to be your school's focus in **all** your communications. That is your 'hero' campaign for this period.

Halo – during this period there will be a halo effect from the focus on your 'hero' campaign that brings a positive impact to **all** of the other departments in the school.

Holistic – check that **all** communication from the school during this period is focused on your 'hero' campaign and critically holistic in both the branding used, and the messaging given. You can do this by literally putting all your marketing materials on one table and checking the consistency.

3-H is an easy way to ensure your campaigns are clear.

It would be really interesting to hear your views about using '3-H' in the higher education world? In addition, I would be interested in hearing about the techniques you use to perfect your campaigns?

Get in touch!

I would love to hear your views on the articles in this book.

You can reach me at Daniel.Cohen@Graduway.com.